THE OILERS

Celebrating Edmonton's Quest
for Lord Stanley's Cup

Fenn Publishing Company Ltd.

THE OILERS:

Celebrating Edmonton's Quest for Lord Stanley's Cup

A Fenn Publishing Book / First Published in 2006

Designed by First Image
Fenn Publishing Company Ltd.
Bolton, Ontario, Canada
Printed in Canada

Acknowledgements
The author would like to thank the few but important people who have made this book come
about. First, to publisher Jordan Fenn for his support and enthusiasm for the project. Next
to the excellent design team of Michael Gray and Rob Scanlan at First Image. Also to Nancy
Glowinski and David Pillinger at Reuters and Craig Campbell and Phil Pritchard at the Hockey
Hall of Fame in Toronto. Without their assistance, this project could not have come to fruition.

All photos courtesy of Reuters,
except pp. 9, 108, 109, 110—courtesy of Hockey Hall of Fame:

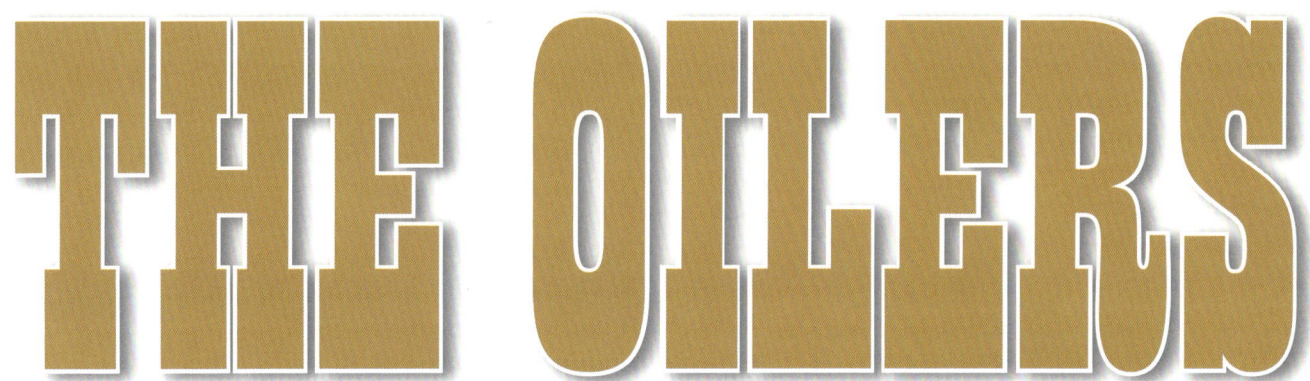

THE OILERS

Celebrating Edmonton's Quest for Lord Stanley's Cup

Fenn Publishing Company Ltd.

Contents

An Edmontonian walks past Rexall Place,
one wall of which is decorated with giant
murals of the team's Stanley Cup rings.

Introduction

Although the Edmonton Oilers started the 2005-06 season in better shape than in recent years, no one could possibly have envisioned a scenario whereby the team would go all the way to game seven of the Stanley Cup finals. It was a dream season, a season that promised more for the future and gave so much of that future up front and in advance. For all the heartbreak of a game-seven loss there was the thrill of a playoff run that no one expected.

Sure, the NHL and players had a new contract which called for a salary cap. Sure, this resulted almost immediately in the team acquiring superstar defenceman Chris Pronger, an enormous piece of any successful puzzle. Sure, the team acquired Michael Peca a day later, another star acquisition. But none of this added up to what actually transpired during this amazing season.

Indeed, the team began the year in a way that suggested it was on the right track, had a ways to go, and would be competitive every night—no more, no less. The Oilers started with a modest but impressive three-game win streak out of the gate, but this was followed by seven losses in a row, the last two by 7–1 and 5–3 scores to Colorado, a team truly in the Stanley Cup mix.

The Oilers ended that horrible streak with an impressive 5–3 win of its own against Dallas, another top team, and this snowballed into a five-game winning streak that gave the team confidence. Much of the next three and a half months leading up to the Turin Olympic break was the same way, however, hot and cold, and this further suggested a team on the way up but by no means at the top.

Inconsistency was the team's greatest problem, and even worse it was inconsistency in goal that undid many a great effort. The goalie tandem of Ty Conklin and Jussi Markannen were amazing some nights, weak other nights. As the trade deadline neared, general manager Kevin Lowe made goaltending his top priority. He acquired Dwayne Roloson from Minnesota on March 8 for a 1st-round and 3rd-round draft choice in 2006. It was a great trade because he got a top-flight goaltender without giving up a roster player, and coming down the stretch it was Roloson's play that gave the team more confidence and took the team into the playoffs.

"Took the team" isn't quite right. The Oilers, in fact, qualified for the post season after the 81st of 82 regular-season games, but they entered the playoffs on a high note, winning their last two games and playing with a sense of purpose.

In the playoffs, they had to face the Presidents' Trophy-winning Detroit Red Wings in the first round, a series that turned on a Jarret Stoll goal midway through the second overtime period of the third game. That gave the Oilers a 2–1 series lead, and although they lost game four, they knew they could win the series if they stuck to their game plan. They did, and by so doing sent the Red Wings packing.

Edmonton picked up momentum in the second round against San Jose. After falling behind 2–0 in that series, they reeled off four wins in a row, Roloson proving spectacular and the team defence able to shut down Joe Thornton and Jonathan Cheechoo, two of the top point-getters of the regular season. Against Anaheim, they were unstoppable, and when they got to the finals, they were facing a Carolina team every bit as happy to be chasing the Cup in the final round.

The big difference was that the Hurricanes were a top team all year; the Oilers were merely a hot team improving as it went along. To make matters worse, Roloson was hurt in game one and lost for the series, and the Oilers had to rely on Makkanen. By the time game four was over, a convincing 2–1 Carolina win which sent the teams back to Raleigh for what would surely be the Cup presentation, the Oilers looked down and out.

Fernando Pisani, however, changed the series entirely when he scored a short-handed goal in overtime to give the Oilers a 4–3 win they richly deserved. In game six, the Oilers dominated, setting up a one-game showdown back in Carolina for the Stanley Cup. They fell one goal short, one shot short, but they discovered they were a more amazing team than they knew. This is a tribute to their season.

Organization

Owners   Edmonton Investors Group Ltd.
   Dave Addie, Neal Allen, Jakob Ambrosius, Manuel Balsa, Ted
   Barrett, Edwin E. Bean, W. Gordon Buchanan, William Butler,
   Michael A. Dalton, The Edmonton Journal, Ernie M. Elko,
   Gary Gregg, Donald T. Hamilton, Ron Hodgson, Jim Hole,
   Gerald Knoll, Chris Kuchar, Larry Makelki, Tom Mason, Todd
   McFarlane, Tim Melton, Art Mihalcheon, Cal Nichols, Brian
   Nilsson, Al Owen, J.R. Paine, Marcel Roberge, Roger Roberge,
   Harold Roozen, Bruce Saville, Dale Sheard, Simon Sochatsky,
   Rusty Stalwick, Keith Weaver, C.J. Woods, Jim Zanello

Governor   Cal Nichols
Alternate Governors   Patrick R. LaForge, Kevin Lowe, William
Butler
President & CEO   Patrick R. LaForge
Executive Vice President & General Manager   Kevin Lowe
Vice President, Hockey Operations   Kevin Prendergast
Assistant General Manager   Scott Howson
Head Coach   Craig MacTavish
Assistant Coaches   Charlie Huddy, Bill Moores, Craig Simpson
Goaltending Coach   Pete Peeters
Video Coach   Brian Ross
Development Coach   Geoff Ward
Director of Research, Analysis,
and Software Development   Sean Draper
Scouting Staff
   Mike Abbamont, Bob Brown, Bill Dandy, Brad Davis, Lorne
   Davis, Morey Gare, Kent Hawley, Stu MacGregor, Chris
   McCarthy, Frank Musil, Kent Nilsson, Dave Semenko, John
   Stevenson
Executive Assistant to the President   Lisa Stanley
Executive Assistant to the General Manager   Valerie Rendell
Security Advisor   Gary Goulet

MEDICAL AND TRAINING STAFF
Head Medical Trainer   Ken Lowe
Assistant Medical Trainer   Kim Layton
Head Equipment Manager   Barrie Stafford
Equipment Manager   Lyle Kulchisky
Assistant Equipment Manager   Jeff Lang
Massage Therapist   Stewart Poirier
Team Medical Chief of Staff   Dr. David C. Reid
Team Physicians   Dr. John Clarke, Dr. Dhiren Naidu
Team Dermatologist   Dr. Don Groot
Team Dentists   Dr. Ben Eastwood, Dr. Tony Sneazwell
Fitness Consultants   Dr. Art Quinney, Dr. Gordon Bell
Physical Therapy Consultant   Dr. Dave Magee
Team Optometrist   Dr. Brent Saik
Special Assignment Conditioning   Daryl Duke

COMMUNICATIONS & BROADCAST
Vice President, Communications & Broadcast   Allan Watt
Manager, Communications & Media Relations   J.J. Hebert
Information Coordinator   Steve Knowles
New Media Production Manager   Andreas Schwabe
New Media Production Coordinator   Marc Ciampa
Director of Broadcast   Don Metz
Game Night Supervisor   Marilyn Riddell
Game Night Director   Glenn Wiun

FINANCE & ADMINISTRATION
Vice President of Finance &
Chief Financial Officer   Darryl Boessenkool
Executive Assistant to the Chief Financial
Officer & Office Manager   Sherry Smith
Controller   Jason Quilley
Assistant Controller   Sangeeta Sundar
Financial Services Coordinator   Corrine McGregor
Payroll Manager   Shawna Quigley
Human Resource Manager   Tandy Kustiak
Accounts Payable Coordinator   Yvonne Weleschuk
Director of Facilities & Events   Craig Tkachuk
IT Manager   Terry Rhoades
Systems Administrator   Rod Pruden

MARKETING & COMMUNICATIONS

Vice President, Marketing   Stew MacDonald
Director, Marketing   Natalie Minckler
Manager, Corporate Communications   Darren Krill
Manager, E—Marketing & Research   Christine Dmytryshyn
Director, Fan Development &
Executive Director, Edmonton Oilers
Community Foundation   Gillian Andries
Coordinator, Fan Development   Sandra Pysklywyc
ICE School Coordinator   Sandy VanRiper
Director, Licensing & Special Projects   Nick Wilson
Director, Operations & Events   Craig Tkachuk
Coordinator, Events   Stacey Brockoff
Coordinator, Operations   Chris Delorey
Receptionists   Cheryl Thomas, Sandy Langley

SALES
Vice President, Sales & Sponsorships   Eric Upton

CORPORATE SALES

Director, Corporate Sales   Brad MacGregor
Corporate Sales Managers   Michael Lake, Daryl Zelinski
Executive Suites Manager   Bob Haromy
Corporate Inventory Specialist   Connie Lloyd
Corporate Sales Coordinators
   Bryce Crittenden, Chris Field, Sangelle Rakowski, Angie Zander

TICKET SALES & SERVICE
Director of Ticket Sales & Service
Sean Price
Sales Administrative Assistant   Lesli Rentz
Sales Account Executives
   Melissa Shave, Sheldon Smart, Tyler Waye, Janice Wimberly
   Client Service Representatives   Terry Bludd, Tabitha Kobeluck,
   Blair McGeough, Stephen Slawuta
Inside Sales Representatives
   Brad Bistritz, Calvin Brown, Abraham Hajar
Group Sales Specialist   James McGregor
Ticket Inventory Manager   Jamie Schenknecht
Credit Supervisor   Patrick Sanders
Customer Service Representative   Kelley Wylie

The Birth of the Edmonton Oilers

It was in large part thanks to the energetic efforts of Bill Hunter, an Edmontonian, that professional hockey got on the map in his hometown in the early 1970s. Hunter owned the Edmonton Oil Kings, the city's junior team, and when news of an expansion league known as the World Hockey Association spread, he was vocal in his interest to bring a team to Edmonton and call it the Oil Kings as well.

The fledgling WHA management group embraced his proposal and saw this team competing fiercely with a Calgary franchise. When the formal announcement was made to start the WHA, late in 1971, both cities were part of the initial league structure. Unfortunately, the Calgary entry was forced to withdraw the following spring, so Hunter decided to use the provincial appellation Alberta Oilers instead. A year later, however, he changed the name to Edmonton Oilers, and it has been that way ever since.

Hunter was a combination of Harold Ballard and John Brophy—loud, abrasive, flamboyant—and not particularly successful at the professional level. In the summer of 1975, because of poor attendance and public weariness of Hunter's personality, he was forced to sell the team to Nelson Skalbania. A year and a half later, the first significant piece of the Oilers' puzzle fell into place when coach Bep Guidolin resigned, in February 1977. Skalbania hired veteran forward Glen Sather to perform the dual roles of player and coach, a task the itinerant fourth-liner performed for half a season before deciding to retire as a player and focus full-time on leading the team from behind the bench.

That summer also saw Skalbania sell the team to Peter Pocklington while he took ownership of the Indianapolis Racers. Skalbania ended up signing 17-year-old Wayne Gretzky to a contract for the 1978–79 season, but just a few games into the new year Skalbania's finances were in such dire straits that he sold Gretzky for $700,000 to Pocklington. Gretzky stepped into the Oilers' lineup and produced record totals for the team. The teen phenom led Edmonton to the Avco Cup finals where the team was defeated by the Winnipeg Jets. It was an ironic season on both these counts because (a) Pocklington would later sell Gretzky to the Los Angeles Kings because of his own financial problems and (b) the Oilers would go on to defeat the Jets in every playoff series the teams contested in the NHL.

After this '78–'79 season, the WHA and the NHL finally made peace. Four teams joined the NHL while the other WHA teams folded and their players claimed by NHL teams in a dispersal draft. An important part of the negotiations of this merger centred around Gretzky. NHL owners wanted all players available in the Dispersal Draft, but the WHA insisted each of its teams—Edmonton, Quebec, Hartford, Winnipeg—be allowed to keep two players, a way of ensuring Gretzky remained with the Oilers and not claimed by an NHL team. The NHL relented, and the rest, as they say, is history. Since the Oilers joined the NHL in the fall of 1979, they have won five Stanley Cups prior to 2006, more than any other team in that time. Glen Sather, as coach and later general manager, was involved in every one of those victories.

Jacques Plante ended his playing career in 1974–75 as a member of the WHA version of the Oilers.

Training Camp Roster

Name	Primary 2005–06 Team
Joel Andresen	Victoria Salmon Kings (ECHL)
Braden Appleby	University of Alberta (CIS)Brett
Arcand-Kootenay	Laredo Bucks (CHL)
Dan Baum	Greenville Grrrowl (ECHL)
Marc-Andre Bergeron	NHL roster
Troy Bodie	Kelowna Rockets (WHL)
Kyle Brodziak	Iowa Stars (AHL)
Ty Conklin	NHL roster
Cory Cross	NHL roster
Travis Cunningham	released
Darren Deschamps	Kalamazoo Wings (UHL)
Nate DiCasmirro	Grand Rapids Griffins (AHL)
Jeff Drouin-Deslauriers	released
Devan Dubnyk	Kamloops Blazers (WHL)
Mike Duco	Kitchener Rangers (OHL)
Radek Dvorak	NHL roster
Mike Gabinet	Idaho Steelheads (ECHL)/ Iowa Stars (AHL)
Kevin Gardner	Idaho Steelheads/ Stockton Thunder (ECHL)
Matt Glasser	Fort McMurray Oil Barons (AJHL)
Stephane Goulet	Moncton Wildcats (QMJHL)
Matt Greene	Iowa Stars (AHL)/ NHL roster
Todd Harvey	NHL roster
Ales Hemsky	NHL roster
Shawn Horcoff	NHL roster
Eric Hunter	Prince George Cougars (WHL)
J.J. Hunter	Hamilton Bulldogs (AHL)
Jean-Francois Jacques	Hamilton Bulldogs (AHL)
Brett Jaeger	Fresno Falcons (ECHL)
Georges Laraque	NHL roster
R.J. Larochelle	Swift Current Broncos (WHL)
Jordan Little	Greenville Grrrowl/ Bakersfield Condors (ECHL)
Jussi Markkanen	NHL roster
Ethan Moreau	NHL roster
Mike Morrison	NHL roster
Michael Peca	NHL roster
Randy Perry	did not play
Toby Petersen	Iowa Stars (AHL)
Fernando Pisani	NHL roster
Jason Platt	Iowa Stars (AHL)
Marc-Antoine Pouliot	Hamilton Bulldogs (AHL)
Chris Pronger	NHL roster
Brock Radunske	Greenville Grrrowl (ECHL)
Marty Reasoner	NHL roster
Liam Reddox	Peterborough Petes (OHL)
Jani Rita	NHL roster
Mathieu Roy	Acadie-Bathurst Titan (QMJHL)
Tony Salmelainen	HIFK Helsinki (Finland)
Rob Schremp	London Knights (OHL)
Alexei Semenov	NHL roster
Tim Sestito	Greenville Grrrowl (ECHL)
Tyler Shantz	did not play
Dan Smith	Hamilton Bulldogs (AHL)
Jason Smith	NHL roster
Kenny Smith	Portland Pirates (AHL)/ Greenville Grrrowl (ECHL)
Ryan Smyth	NHL roster
Aaron Sorochan	University of Alberta (CIS)
Tyler Spurgeon	Kelowna Rockets (WHL)
Steve Staios	NHL roster
Yan Stastny	Iowa Stars (AHL)
Jarret Stoll	NHL roster
Zack Stortini	Iowa Stars/ Milwaukee Admirals (AHL)
Danny Syvret	Hamilton Bulldogs (AHL)
Adam Taylor	Victoria Salmon Kings (ECHL)
Roman Tesliuk	Kamloops Blazers (WHL)
Raffi Torres	NHL roster
Slava Trukhno	PEI Rocket (QMJHL)
Igor Ulanov	NHL roster
Brad Winchester	Hamilton Bulldogs (AHL)
Colton Yellow Horn	released
Bryan Young	Peterborough Petes (OHL)

Goalie Devan Dubyk was drafted by the Oilers and was a member of Canada's National Junior Team Development Camp in August 2005 before going to Edmonton for his first NHL camp.

Colorado goalie David Aebischer stops this chance by Shawn Horcoff, but moments later Horcoff scored his team's first goal of the season for an early 1–0 lead.

October 5, 2005
Colorado 3 at **Edmonton 4**

Playing their first game in a year and a half before a sellout crowd of 16,839, the Oilers started their season faster than any other in team history. Shawn Horcoff scored just 25 seconds from the opening faceoff to give his team a 1–0 lead, but the rest of the game was not so easy. The Avs tied the game five minutes later, but Ryan Smyth restored the lead at 6:16 when he tipped a Radek Dvorak shot past goalie David Aebischer. Colorado tied the game a second time on a goal by Antti Laaksonen midway through the period, but in the second Jarret Stoll scored the lone goal and the Oilers had another one-goal lead. This was a period dominated by Edmonton as it fired 14 shots at Aebischer while Ty

Conklin faced two harmless shots in the Oilers' net. Again, however, they let the advantage slip away, this time midway through the third. It was up to Horcoff to finish the scoring and bookend a memorable game for himself as he netted the winner at 16:32. Smyth had a goal and two assists, and the Oilers outshot the visitors 31–17.

October 8, 2005
Vancouver 3 at **Edmonton 4** (SO)

It was the first of eight meetings between these division and geographic rivals, and the Oilers came out on top in an exciting, dramatic, and penalty-filled game that saw five of the six regulation goals scored over the course of 19 power

plays. In the end, it was a shootout—the first for both teams—that settled the score. For the second game in a row, Shawn Horcoff scored early to put the Oilers out in front, and again a familiar pattern emerged as they gave up the next goal to nullify that early lead. Raffi Torres, celebrating his 24th birthday, scored the only goal of the second period with the extra man, but Markus Naslund scored 5-on-4 early in the third to tie the game again. The Canucks went ahead midway through the period, and Torres tied the game on another power play with just 23 seconds left in regulation. The five-minute overtime settled nothing, so players went to their benches to prepare for the shootout. Torres finished his birthday present to himself by scoring on the first shot for Edmonton after Naslund

Ethan Moreau tries a wraparound off his backhand while goalie Jason LaBarbera keeps his paddle down and defenceman Lubomir Visnovsky tries to check him.

had missed, and Ales Hemsky sealed the game when he scored on his penalty shot.

October 10, 2005
Edmonton 4 at Anaheim 2

The Oilers continued their perfect start to the season with their third straight win, this a narrow decision on the road augmented by an empty-net goal in the final minute. For the second consecutive game, Raffi Torres scored twice in a game which saw the Oilers rally from 2–0 down after the first period. All three of their goals before the empty netter came on the power play. Torres and Marty Reasoner scored the only two markers of the second to tie the score, and Edmonton pulled ahead midway through the third when Radek Dvorak scored with two extra men while Teemu Selanne and Keith Carney were in the box for the Ducks. At the other end of special teams, the Oilers were perfect, killing all seven short-handed situations. Ryan Smyth missed the game for Edmonton because of a sprained knee and Todd Harvey sat out with a bruised foot.

October 11, 2005
Edmonton 1 at **Los Angeles 3**

The Oilers concluded their two-game swing through California with their first loss of the year. Penalties were the main culprit this night, in part because they allowed two Kings goals on the power play, in part because they were short-handed ten times, making it difficult to establish any flow or momentum off good shifts. Joe Corvo put Los Angeles on the board midway through the first, but Marc-Andre Bergeron scored his first of the season a short time later to tie the game. Dustin Brown scored the only goal of the second when he banked a shot off the skate of goalie Ty Conklin, and Eric Belanger dimmed Edmonton's hopes with a goal early in the third. It was another bad goal as Conklin failed to hold a weak shot by Sean Avery and Belanger banged home the loose puck. The Kings outshot Edmonton 10–4 in the third and three penalties by the Oilers didn't help matters.

Brad Winchester attempts to stuff the puck in, but goalie Miikka Kiprusoff is there to make the save as defenceman Bryan Marchment takes Winchester.

when his go-ahead goal midway through the period held up and the Stars swept their two Alberta games against Calgary and Edmonton. The Oilers took only two minor penalties all night, but they came up empty on five power plays of their own, a sure sign of trouble in the new NHL. Hedberg improved his career record against Edmonton to 4–0–0.

October 15, 2005
Edmonton 0 at **Calgary 3**

Round One of the 2005–06 edition of the Battle of Alberta went to the Flames, but going into the game both teams were playing with less than full confidence. The Oilers had lost two in a row and Calgary its last three, but the home team got rid of the butterflies in the first period by jumping out into a 2–0 lead courtesy of goals from Daymond Langkow and Jarome Iginla. Langkow hammered in a loose puck, and Iginla stole the puck from Cory Cross and beat Jussi Markkanen through the pads. The Oilers stormed Miikka Kiprusoff's crease in the second, but the Finnish goalie was superb in blocking all 15 shots he faced in that 20 minutes. Rhett Warrener closed out the scoring with a goal into the empty net. For the second consecutive game the Oilers' power play drew blanks, this time going 0–8 with the extra man. Markkanen, who had played well in relief of Ty Conklin the previous night, got the start and stopped 25 of 28 Calgary shots. The loss pulled Edmonton back to .500, a promising 3–0–0 start to the year giving way to three straight losses.

October 14, 2005
Dallas 3 at Edmonton 2

For the third straight game the Oilers found themselves trailing in the first period, and for the second time they couldn't get a win. This night, however, they were the better team. The Stars led 2–0 early in the second thanks to goals by Jussi Jokinen and Bill Guerin, and soon after that second one coach Craig MacTavish decided to shake up his bench by pulling Ty Conklin and inserting Jussi Markkanen into the nets. The strategy worked as the Oilers scored once in the second and then Jani Rita's marker early in the third period tied the game at 2–2 as he tipped a point shot from Marc-Andre Bergeron past goalie Johan Hedberg. Steve Ott proved the hero for Dallas, though,

October 18, 2005
Phoenix 4 at Edmonton 3 (OT)

This was the first visit to Edmonton by Wayne Gretzky as coach of the Coyotes, and the arena in Edmonton was trembling with excitement. The Oilers held a special ceremony to retire defenceman Paul Coffey's number 7 before the game, and the team appropriately chose a night his great teammate Gretzky would be in the building. Again a slow start cost the Oilers, though. Oleg Saprykin scored twice for Phoenix midway through the first period—both on backhands—and Edmonton was again down by two goals heading to the dressing room after 20 minutes. Igor Ulanov scored in the second to draw the team to within one, but Shane Doan restored the two-goal cushion early in the third. The Oilers then mounted a furious rally, outplaying the Desert Dogs and tying the game thanks to two quick goals from Michael Peca and Marty Reasoner soon after Doan's goal. The brief break between the third period and overtime gave Phoenix a chance to recover, and it was the visitors who poured it on in the extra period, scoring on a power play with Steve Staios in the box for a penalty that had carried over from the end of regulation time. Another former Oilers, goalie Curtis Joseph, earned the 399th win of his career while Jussi Markkanen was the losing netminder.

Paul Coffey wipes away the tears during an emotional ceremony prior to the game retiring his number 7 to the rafters.

October 20, 2005
Edmonton 1 at **Calgary 3**

For the fifth straight game the Oilers wound up on the losing end of the score, this time a 3–1 count to Calgary, the second loss to their provincial rivals in a week. Each loss was recorded with Ryan Smyth in the press box with a sore knee. It was the Oilers that struck first this time, a late Ethan Moreau wraparound goal sending his team to the dressing room up a goal after the first period. The Flames got the only two goals of the second, however, both coming late to take the steam out of the Edmonton attack. Steve Reinprecht scored on the power play at 17:12 and just over a minute later Chuck Kobasew put the Flames ahead to stay when he batted the puck out of midair and past Jussi Markkanen. Kobasew added his second of the night late in the third after video review confirmed his shot from in tight slipped over the goal line. Special teams were the difference again, the nearly impotent Oilers' power play going goalless, this time on six chances, while the Flames scored once with the extra man. The win pulled Calgary even with Edmonton for third spot in the Northwest Division with seven points each.

Goalie Jussi Markkanen and defenceman Cory Cross prevent Colorado rookie Wojtek Wolski (out of frame) from scoring.

October 25, 2005
Edmonton 3 at **Colorado 5**

The road end of a home-and-home series with Colorado went only marginally better for Edmonton, the losers of seven straight after this 5–3 defeat at the Pepsi Center. A scoreless first period gave way to four goals in the second, evenly distributed. Colorado jumped into a 2–0 lead early, but Marc-Andre Bergeron and Marty Reasoner tied the game before the second intermission. Raffi Torres, with his team-best sixth goal, put the Oilers in front at 4:12 of the third, as his harmless backhand beat goalie David Aebischer. The Avs tied the game a few minutes later when Alex Tanguay beat Jussi Markkanen on an equally bad goal. Tanguay was behind the Edmonton goal and simply flipped the puck out front. It banked in off Radek Dvorak and past Markkanen who didn't see the puck at all. Just as it seemed the game was heading to overtime, though, Colorado scored twice, in the final minute, to seal the victory. The crippling blow was a slapshot by Patrice Brisebois, playing in his 800th career game, that flew over the blocker side of Markkanen. Steve Konowalchuk put an exclamation mark on the evening with the final goal 29 seconds from the final horn.

October 21, 2005
Colorado 7 at Edmonton 1

The early part of the season was quickly spiraling out of control for Edmonton, this horrible loss the team's sixth straight defeat and the most lop-sided loss at that. The return of Ryan Smyth was of little help, and he played at well below 100 per cent in an effort to get the team back on track. This was no contest from the get-go. Sylvain Turgeon scored early for Colorado, and by the first intermission the Avs were ahead 3–0 and outshooting the Oilers 16–6. After that third goal, Jussi Markkanen was pulled and Ty Conklin sent in, but Markkanen returned to the crease to start the third after Colorado scored four unanswered goals in the middle period. Ethan Moreau ruined David Aebischer's shutout with a power-play goal midway through the third. It was only the team's second power-play score in its previous 37 man-advantage opportunities. Colorado, meanwhile, cashed in on three of eight chances with the extra man.

October 28, 2005
Edmonton 5 at Dallas 3

The Oilers finally got back into the win column, registering their first victory since October 10 with this hard-fought and dramatic victory over Dallas. This night it was the Oilers that built a 2–0 lead early in the second, but Dallas scored two goals in 30 seconds to tie the game. Ryan Smyth showed why he is the team's heart and soul, though, scoring the go-ahead goal late in the period to renew the fragile confidence of a

Radek Dvorak's shot eludes Dallas goalie Marty Turco in the third period for what turned out to be the game-winning score.

team mired in a seven-game losing skein. The Stars tied the game early in the third when Brenden Morrow scored with Steve Staios and Cory Cross in the penalty box, but Edmonton came back again. Radek Dvorak put the Oilers ahead for good at 8:12 when he took a pass from Ethan Moreau in the slot and blasted the puck home. Raffi Torres added a late goal to ensure the victory. Both teams were a weak 1–7 on the power play, and the arena in Dallas was well below capacity.
October 29, 2005

Edmonton 5 at Nashville 1

Buoyed by their win the previous night, the Oilers tackled the previously unbeaten Nashville Predators (8–0–0) and came away with an important victory. Martin Erat scored the first goal early in the game with a snap shot over the glove of Jussi Markkanen to give the surprising Predators the early lead, but the rest of the game was dominated by Edmonton. Ryan Smyth tied the score a few minutes later when he scooped up a rebound after Tomas Vokoun had made a great save on Marc-Andre Bergeron on a breakaway. Bergeron scored the go-ahead goal early in the second, and then the power play finally started to click. The final three Oilers' goals all came with the extra man, and they finished the game going 3–6 on the power play while limiting Nashville to just one goal on seven opportunities. Markkanen got the win for Edmonton and Vokoun (7–1–1) lost for the first time.

Raffi Torres beats Chris Osgood in overtime to give the Oilers a dramatic 4–3 win at the Joe Louis Arena.

November 1, 2005
Columbus 1 at **Edmonton 5**

Playing as they did to start the season, the Oilers won their third straight game for the second time, this win moving them back into a tie for third place in their division. The teams were tied 1–1 after the first, a lucky score for the Blue Jackets who had been badly outplayed during the first 20 minutes. The Oilers didn't give up and stormed the goal of Marc Denis with equal fervour in the second, and they were rewarded with early and late power-play goals from Ales Hemsky and Ryan Smyth, respectively. Two quick goals early in the third solidified the score, one of which was Raffi Torres's eighth goal of the season, fourth highest in the league to date.

November 3, 2005
Edmonton 4 at Detroit 3 (OT)

The Oilers extended their winning ways to four games, this time at the expense of the mighty Detroit Red Wings who had won their last nine games. The winning goal came in overtime and was the result of some great work between Raffi Torres and Steve Staios. Staios put the puck on Torres's stick as he was going to the net, and Torres merely redirected it past Chris Osgood at 1:51 to give the Oilers their biggest win of the season. The teams exchanged goals in each of the three periods of regulation, and in every instance it was the Oilers who went ahead only to lose the lead to the Wings. In the first, it was Shawn Horcoff who spotted the visitors the early lead with a shot that beat Osgood through the legs; in the second, it was Ryan Smyth who

Ryan Smyth beats Patrick Lalime with a deke to the backhand on a penalty shot in the second period during the Oilers' impressive 7–2 win over the Blues.

tipped a great pass from Ales Hemsky into the open side; and, in the third, it was native Edmontonian Fernando Pisani who redirected Chris Pronger's point shot past Osgood. Pronger had assists on two of those goals.

November 4, 2005
Edmonton 7 at St. Louis 2

The Oilers made their biggest move of the early season by handing lowly St. Louis a sound beating. It was their fifth win in a row and one in which everything worked well. Edmonton went 2–6 on the power play and shut down the Blues on eight manpower situations, giving St. Louis its seventh straight loss. Jarret Stoll was the big gun this night scoring twice and adding two assists, his first career four-point game. He got things going with a goal just 1:45 after the opening faceoff on the team's first shot, and Alexei Semenov's first of the year made it 2–0 a few minutes later. The Blues got on the board before the end of the period, but Edmonton scored two unanswered goals in the second to take control. The second of those came from Ryan Smyth on a penalty shot as he beat Patrick Lalime cleanly midway through the second. Reinhard Divis started the third for the Blues, but he didn't fare much better, allowing three more Edmonton goals on just 13 shots.

November 7, 2005
Edmonton 0 at **Dallas 4**

Feeling as though the time was right, coach Craig MacTavish decided that with the team in the middle of a five-game winning streak it was a good chance to play goalie Mike Morrison for the first time in the rookie's career. Morrison wasn't awful, but he didn't provide the same kind of goaltending as Jussi Markkanen had in building the streak to five. Still, his teammates didn't help, firing just 16 shots on Marty Turco who had a relatively easy time in recording his 22nd career shutout. The Stars scored twice in the first period, and it turned out this was all the scoring they'd need. Stephane Robidas added his first of the year in the second on a nice backhand and Mike Modano added his seventh in the third when he banged home a rebound to close out the scoring. Junior Lessard scored his first NHL goal in the opening period for Dallas. Michael Peca missed the game with a concussion.

Edmonton forward Kyle Brodziak is stopped by Nashville goalie Tomas Vokoun early in the third period of the Predators' 3–2 win.

November 8, 2005
Edmonton 2 at **Nashville 3**

The streaky Oilers lost for the second straight game, unable to answer a loss with a win right away. As a result, their 8–8–1 record had them back in the basement of the Northwest Division. It was a game the Oilers should have won, or at least earned a point. Despite a scoreless first period, they were the better team, but it wasn't until midway through the second that they were rewarded for their play. Jarret Stoll scored on the power play at 9:22 with Dan Hamhuis in the penalty box, and this lead held up until early in the third when Martin Erat tied the game. The final two minutes provided a wild and unpredictable ending. Kimmo Timonen scored the go-ahead goal at 18:05 in a flurry of activity around the goal of Jussi Markkanen, seemingly the winning goal. The Oilers came right back, though, and Ryan Smyth tied the game at 19:01, surely the goal to send the game into overtime. But, no! Scott Hartnell managed to get the puck past Markkanen at 19:37, and with just 23 seconds left on the clock the Oilers were out of miracles. They outplayed Nashville most of the night, but a 1–7 performance on the power play was again the difference.

November 11, 2005
Edmonton 3 at Columbus 1

A tight victory that provided a real test for the Oilers, this 3–1 win over Columbus had plenty for the team to use to help establish its identity. First, it snapped a two-game losing streak, nipping bad habits in the bud, as it were. Second, it showed the importance of goaltending as Jussi Markkanen was razor sharp for the Oilers, stopping 29 of 30 shots, several of those in the final minute with Marc Denis on the bench and six Blue Jackets pressing for the tying goal in a 2–1 game. Lastly, it was a tight-checking game. Captain and defenceman Jason Smith scored a rare goal to start the evening, and former Oilers forward Todd Marchant tied the game later in the period. A goalless second set up a tense final period that was played without a penalty either way. Fernando Pisani scored the decisive second goal at 7:36 after a great play by Ales Hemsky to take a hit and make a pass. Radek Dvorak added an empty netter to relieve the pressure. Ryan Smyth assisted on all Oilers goals, and Shawn Horcoff had two helpers. The win gave Edmonton a 9–0–3 record in its last 12 meetings with the Blue Jackets, including a 5–1 win on November 1.

Georges Laraque has an empty net and the puck on his stick but defenceman Duncan Keith makes a great play to prevent a goal.

November 13, 2005
Edmonton 1 at **Chicago 3**

The first period was all that Chicago needed to beat Edmonton this night—that and some fine penalty killing. The Hawks scored all three of their goals in the first 20 minutes, including goals on their first two shots. The Oilers were the better team most of the night, but goalie Jussi Markkanen, making his 14th start for Edmonton, was not at his best. The Edmonton power play was a dismal 0–8 as well. Mark Bell had two of Chicago's goals and missed two good chances with the empty net near the end of the game to get the hat trick. His first goal was a weak one for Markkanen to give up, a long wrist shot that fooled the goalie. The loss dropped the Oilers back to .500 (9–9–1). They had three chances with the extra man in each of the second and third periods but could mount little attack on Chicago goalie Nikolai Khabibulin who stopped 27 shots for the shutout. Markkanen faced just 19 shots from the Hawks. The lone Edmonton goal came off Fernando Pisani's stick on a second-period breakaway.

November 14, 2005
Edmonton 5 at Colorado 2

Bouncing back from the previous night, Edmonton moved ahead of Colorado into third place in the Northwest Division with this convincing win over the Avs to finish a grueling, seven-game road trip. Mike Morrison spotted Jussi Markkanen in goal for Edmonton and won his first career game. Ryan Smyth got Edmonton on the board first, midway through the opening period with a power play wrist shot from the slot, and Ethan Moreau made it 2–0 less than a minute later when Jarret Stoll's pass banked off Moreau's skate and in. The Avs chipped away, though, and got to within a goal on a late power-play marker from defenceman Rob Blake. They tied it in the second, but Chris Pronger scored his first goal of the year for Edmonton, on a power play slapshot from the top of the circle, to make it 3–2 for the Oilers at the second intermission. Despite pressing, the Avs lost ground in the third as Edmonton scored the only two goals of the final 20 minutes. Both teams scored twice with the extra man.

Goalie Chris Osgood loses his plastic neck protector as Ales Hemsky's first-period shot beats him for the game's opening goal.

November 17, 2005
Detroit 5 at **Edmonton 6** (OT)

In what was one of the wildest and most entertaining games of the entire 2005–06 regular season, the Oilers beat Detroit for the second time in overtime this year. Both teams had two-goal leads they squandered; both teams rallied. In the end, it was a Jarret Stoll power-play goal just 33 seconds into the extra period that gave the Oilers a win at Rexall Place before another packed house. Edmonton opened the scoring in the first thanks to Ales Hemsky on the power play as he one-timed a cross-ice pass from Chris Pronger on a 5-on-3. Mikael Samuelsson tied the game after intercepting a Pronger pass and ripping a shot past Jussi Markkanen. In the second, the Red Wings opened a two-goal lead, but the Oilers exploded in the third period for four goals in a span of 6:55. Ryan Smyth had two of that number, and with less than five minutes to play

the Oilers had a 5–3 lead. It wasn't enough. Brendan Shanahan scored at 16:40 with the extra man and captain Steve Yzerman tied the game at 17:42. Just before the end of regulation time, though, Kirk Maltby incurred a goalie interference penalty and that set the stage for Stoll's heroics in the OT. Shawn Horcoff tied a team record (held by Wayne Gretzky) with four assists in that third period flurry for the Oilers.

November 19, 2005
Chicago 4 at Edmonton 3

The Oilers fell short in attempting to duplicate their wild rally two nights previous against Detroit, this time falling behind 4–1 to Chicago but failing to tie the game with third-period heroics. The teams were tied 1–1 after the first period thanks to Edmontonian Rene Bourque (playing for Chicago) and Ales Hemsky of the Oilers, but it was all Chicago in the

second. The Hawks scored the only two goals of the middle period and added another early in the third to build that 4–1 lead. That goal spelled the end for Jussi Markkanen and Mike Morrison finished the game for Edmonton. Chicago tried to sit on the lead the rest of the way and almost blew it. Edmonton scored twice on the power play to make it 4–3, but then the Oilers took two late penalties in the second half of the period to kill their momentum. They were just 2–10 with the extra man while the Hawks were 1–6.

November 21, 2005
San Jose 1 at **Edmonton 2** (SO)

The night's activities began with a special pre-game ceremony which saw the Oilers replace all their banners with modern versions. On ice, though, the game was hardly an updated model of the high-flying Oilers that set all kinds of scoring records in the 1980s. Indeed, the Sharks were mired in a five-game losing streak that went to six by the time this game was over, and the Oilers were playing their sixth game in eleven days. Both of the game's regulation goals came in the second period, the Sharks striking first on a power play, with Patrick Marleau doing the damage, the Oilers coming right back on a Marty Reasoner goal at 19:22 of the period. Overtime yielded nothing, so the teams went to a shootout. Niko Dimitrakos missed for San Jose, as did Raffi Torres for the Oilers. Jonathan Cheechoo missed again for San Jose, but Ales Hemsky beat Evgeni Nabokov to give the Oilers the edge. Marco Sturm made things interesting by scoring on Mike Morrison with the Sharks' third shot, leaving it up to Ryan Smyth to score and win or miss and keep the shootout going. Smyth made no mistake, and the 16,583 fans went home happy.

Edmonton's Fernando Pisani fights for the puck with the Sharks' Jonathan Cheechoo.

November 23, 2005
Edmonton 4 at Minnesota 3

Ethan Moreau was the hero in Minnesota as he scored the game-winning goal with just 50 seconds left in the third period when his quick shot in the slot hit defenceman Filip Kuba and deflected past goalie Dwayne Roloson. The win, coupled with Colorado's 7–3 loss to Detroit, put Edmonton alone in third place in the Northwest Division. Raffi Torres scored his 11th goal of the season just 2:10 into the game to give Edmonton the early lead but the Wild struck for two goals midway through the period to take a 2–1 lead. Ales Hemsky tied the game for the Oilers less than two minutes later and the game settled into a close-checking affair. The Oilers seemed to take control on a Jarret Stoll goal midway through the second as his wrist shot was only partially stopped by Roloson before falling into the net, but Pascal Dupuis tied the game early in the third. He took a great pass from Pierre-Marc Bouchard, faked a shot to draw goalie Mike Morrison out of position ever so slightly, and then ripped a shot home. Both teams had power-play chances in the final period but neither could capitalize. It was up to Moreau to score the winner as the game seemed destined for overtime. Morrison improved his record to 3–0–0 to begin his NHL career as a backup to Jussi Markkanen.

He may be on his knees, but Calgary goalie Miikka Kiprusoff is square to the shooter, Radek Dvorak, and makes the second-period save.

November 25, 2005
Edmonton 2 at Calgary 1 (SO)

The Oilers improved their record to 14–10–1 with this shootout win over Calgary at the Pengrowth Saddledome. Fernando Pisani scored the winning goal in the first sudden-death round of the penalty shot competition to make amends for his team losing a 1–0 lead in the third period. Radek Dvorak got the Oilers in front at 14:42 of the first period after one-timing a nice pass from Jarret Stoll, and that lead held up for the next 35 minutes. It wasn't until midway through the third period that Marcus Nilson tied the game for the Flames. It was the Oilers, however, that had the best chance to win in overtime. They began the extra period up a man as Roman Hamrlik had taken a hooking penalty at 19:48 of the third, but Edmonton could not capitalize with the extra man, and the game went to the shootout. Raffi Torres, Ales Hemsky, and Ryan Smyth all missed for Edmonton and Tony Amonte, Jarome Iginla, and defenceman Dion Phaneuf missed for Calgary. That set the stage for the one-on-one shootout, and Pisani buried his opportunity with a nice deke before sliding the puck between Miikka Kiprusoff's legs. Chuck Kobasew had a chance to tie for the hometown Flames, but Mike Morrison made the save to preserve the win. He improved his record to 4–0–0 while Kiprusoff fell to 12–7–3.

November 29, 2005
Colorado 3 at Edmonton 2

A four-day layoff did as much harm as good for Edmonton, which looked a little rusty playing a Colorado team that had played two nights earlier. Still, the Oilers were the better team and were unfortunate not to come away with at least a point. The Avs jumped out to a 2–0 lead by the first intermission despite having just four shots, both goals coming from Ian Laperriere, but Edmonton fought back. Marc-Andre Bergeron made it 2–1 early in the second and Michael Peca tied the count at 9:29 with his first goal in 14 games. Joe Sakic scored the only goal of the third, his second successive game winner. He beat Mike Morrison with one of his quick, hard snapshots in the slot. The Oilers pressed for the tying goal with Morrison on the bench, but to no avail. Morrison lost for the first time in his young career (4–1–0). Edmonton lost for the first time in four games despite outshooting Colorado 31–17.

December 1, 2005
Vancouver 3 at **Edmonton 5**

Bouncing back from a loss two nights earlier, the Oilers dominated much of the game against division-leading Vancouver and with the victory moved to within three points of first place. Although the Canucks scored just 18 seconds from the opening faceoff off a Josh Green shot, it was Edmonton that had the better scoring chances the rest of this penalty-free period. Jarret Stoll tied the game at 8:25 and just over two minutes later Marty Reasoner scored his sixth of the year to give the Oilers a lead they never surrendered. The teams exchanged goals in the second, Ryan Smyth scoring early to open a 3–1 lead on a nice backhand. Daniel Sedin made it a one-goal game again at 14:49 on

Spray flies as defenceman Cory Cross controls the puck after the initial save by goalie Jussi Markkanen. Boston's Marco Sturm can't get to it.

the power play with Michael Peca in the box for high-sticking. Raffi Torres and Stoll made it 5–2 in the third, at which point Vancouver coach Marc Crawford pulled goalie Alex Auld and inserted Rob McVicar who made his NHL debut. Stoll's goal was a long shot that Auld should have saved easily. McVicar played just 2:44 before being pulled for the extra attacker. This turned out to be his only NHL time all year. A late Anson Carter goal made the score a bit more respectable.

December 3, 2005
Boston 5 at Edmonton 4 (OT)

David Tanabe's goal with just 30 seconds left in the overtime gave the Bruins a 5–4 win and sent the Rexall Place fans home disappointed this night. It was a game the Oilers felt they should have won because by the 4:33 mark of the second period

they were leading 3–0 and were in complete control. Then the roof fell in and the Bruins scored the next four goals. It was Edmonton that had to rally in the third to tie the game. Todd Harvey on a wraparound and Ryan Smyth on a rebound scored late in the first to start the scoring for the Oilers, and Fernando Pisani added one early in the second to put the game in the Oilers' hands. Brad Boyes scored twice, though, sandwiched around a Sergei Samsonov goal midway through the second, and by the time the teams went to the dressing room after 40 minutes the Bruins were flying and the Oilers were upset at themselves for blowing a three-goal lead. In the third, Patrice Bergeron scored just 13 seconds from the start of the period before Pisani tied the game at 3:46. The win was the second in a row for Boston since trading Joe Thornton to San Jose a few days earlier.

Ethan Moreau goes in alone on goalie Antero Niittymaki and scores his second short-handed goal of the game, in the second period. This proved to be the game winner.

December 8, 2005
Edmonton 3 at Philadelphia 2

Special teams made all the difference tonight, but given the Oilers' weak power play it was the penalty killers who left their mark on the game. More specifically, Ethan Moreau scored two goals short-handed and Edmonton added its third goal with the extra man. The Flyers had eight power plays but scored only once and allowed the two goals against, not a good ratio by any means. Still, they kept the game close despite being without several top players including Peter Forsberg, Keith Primeau, Eric Desjardins, Joni Pitkanen, and goalie Robert Esche. As a result of the latter, Antero Niittymaki got the start for the Flyers but he was by no means the reason they lost. Moreau scored the only goal of the first period

with his captain Jason Smith in the penalty box. Early in the second Branko Radivojevic tied the game, but the Oilers scored twice more before the period ended to take a 3–1 lead to the third. Jarret Stoll scored on a backhand on the power play and Moreau, this time with Michael Peca in the box, scored his second goal 4-on-5. His initial shot was stopped by Niittymaki, but Moreau followed up and knocked in his own rebound.

December 10, 2005
Edmonton 2 at **NY Islanders 3** (SO)

There were good and bad things to come out of this game, a shootout loss on Long Island. On the good, the Oilers rallied late in the third to earn a point in the standings. The bad was that they blew an early lead

and were a woeful 1–9 on the power play. Fernando Pisani missed on his shootout attempt and Alexei Yashin scored, and then Ales Hemsky scored for the Oilers while Jussi Markkanen stopped Jason Blake to bring the game down to one shot for both teams. Rick DiPietro stoned Ryan Smyth, though, and Trent Hunter made no mistake, giving the Islanders the shootout victory. The Oilers scored the lone goal of the first period thanks to Pisani, but the Islanders tied the game in the second and went ahead midway through the third on a Hunter power-play goal. Defenceman Chris Pronger tied the game on an Edmonton man advantage at 18:56, the team's first goal with the extra man after being ineffective the rest of the night on eight previous chances. He took an Ales Hemsky feed in the slot and let

New Jersey goalie Martin Brodeur stops Ales Hemsky during the shootout to give the Devils a victory.

go a wrist shot that beat DiPietro cleanly. Edmonton was forced to survive overtime when Shawn Horcoff took a penalty midway through, but the Oilers ran out of breaks in the penalty shot contest.

December 13, 2005
Edmonton 1 at **New Jersey 2** (SO)

For the second straight game the Oilers lost in a shootout, and for the second straight time they got to the shootout after killing off a minor penalty to Shawn Horcoff in the five-minute overtime. This time they were fortunate to come away with a point. Richard Matvichuk scored the only goal of the first period and defenceman Cory Cross scored his second goal of the year in the middle period to tie the game. The story was the Edmonton penalty killers, though, as they blanked the Devils on nine manpower advantages. Ethan Moreau had the best chance to break the tie when he hit the post

in the third, and in overtime it was all New Jersey. The Devils outshot Edmonton 6–1 but couldn't beat Ty Conklin who almost single-handedly earned a point for the Oilers tonight. In the shootout, though, New Jersey had more success. Jarret Stoll and Ales Hemsky both couldn't get the puck past Martin Brodeur, but Slava Kozlov on the deke and Brain Gionta with a nice backhand both scored for the Devils to give them the extra point.

December 15, 2005
Montreal 3 at **Edmonton 5**

In one of the most important stretches of games of the season for Edmonton, the Oilers won the first of five key games that launched them to success the rest of the year. Although they got the game's first goal, a power-play marker from Marc-Andre Bergeron, it was their comeback a bit later that defined the team's character. Montreal scored the next

three goals, the last of which at 4:08 from Chris Higgins early in the second put the Canadiens in control. The Oilers refused to succumb, and from that point forward they dominated. Ty Conklin was in net for the second straight game and faced only six shots over the final two periods. Raffi Torres scored his 13th of the year a minute after the Higgins goal to bring the score to 3–2, and the Oilers tied the game early in the third. Ethan Moreau scored the game winner late in the final period. More important, it came on a power play. He blasted a slapshot over the shoulder of Jose Theodore in the Montreal net at 18:47, and Fernando Pisani added one into the empty net to close out the scoring. Jarret Stoll, the team's leading scorer, had one assist to bring his points total to 28. Montreal was without three of its best players—captain Saku Koivu, right winger Alexei Kovalev, and centreman Radek Bonk.

This third-period opportunity by Vancouver's Todd Bertuzzi looks like a sure thing, but goalie Jussi Markkanen makes a great save on the play.

December 17, 2005
Edmonton 5 at Vancouver 4 (OT)

Perhaps this was the biggest win of the season to date. It sure was a character builder, as they say, and it sure provided the Oilers with some confidence as they edged ever closer to first-place Vancouver in the Northwest Division standings. Vancouver built a 2–0 lead by 7:03 of the first, and sensing trouble coach Craig MacTavish took out starter Mike Morrison in favour of Jussi Markkanen to wake up his bench. Ryan Smyth responded with a power-play goal a few minutes later, and Ales Hemsky tied the game in the second with another goal 5-on-4. Not to be outdone, Todd Bertuzzi and Anson Carter put the Canucks up by two once again, but the third period was all Edmonton. The Oilers scored twice more to

send the game into overtime, Marty Reasoner scoring first. Shawn Horcoff then took a pass from Ethan Moreau and ripped a slapshot past Maxime Ouellet. Michael Peca was the hero at 4:08 of the extra period when he beat Ouellet on a backhand to give the Oilers two points. Edmonton went 3–11 on the power play while holding the Canucks goalless on six chances.

December 19, 2005
Calgary 4 at Edmonton 5

The Oilers won for the third straight game and moved into a tie for second place with the Flames, both teams having 42 points. The win also moved Edmonton to within two points of Vancouver for first place in the division. They got the two points thanks to a series of

rallies and a never-say-die attitude that was too much for the Flames to handle. Calgary went up early in the first; Edmonton tied the game. The Flames went up 2–1; Edmonton tied the game again before the first intermission. In the second, the Flames went up 4–2, but the Oilers drew to within one before 40 minutes was up. In the third, the Oilers took over, outshooting Calgary 15–7 and scoring twice. Shawn Horcoff tied the game midway through the period and Fernando Pisani scored the winner at 19:15 to climax a dramatic comeback. For the second straight game, coach Craig MacTavish made a goaltending change, this at 5:51 of the second when the Flames went up 3–2. Mike Morrison came out, and although Jussi Markkanen allowed a goal on the first shot he faced, he was perfect thereafter and gave the Oilers a chance to win.

December 21, 2005
Edmonton 7 at Vancouver 6

The Oilers won their fourth game in a row, but for the third straight time they required a goaltending change to get the job done. Still, the story this night was the team's relentless attack and optimistic attitude regardless the situation. They scored the first goal early, but soon found themselves trailing 2–1. They tied the game four times before finally taking the lead in the third for good. Shawn Horcoff tied the score 2–2 late in the first. In the second, Vancouver had leads of 3–2, 4–3, and 5–4, but every time the Oilers found a way to get the goal back. Ales Hemsky, Michael Peca, and Raffi Torres all scored before the end of the second to make it 5–5. Ryan Smyth and Marty Reasoner put the Oilers up for keeps midway through the third and Daniel Sedin made the game a bit closer in the final minute. Vancouver scored five of its six goals on the power play, and the Oilers converted two of their six man-advantage opportunities. The win moved Edmonton into a tie with Vancouver for top spot in the division, both teams having won 20 games. Calgary was just two points behind.

December 23, 2005
Los Angeles 3 at Edmonton 5

Edmonton pulled ahead of Vancouver by one point for top spot in the division with its fifth win in a row, a home victory dominated by power plays in the final game before Christmas. Both teams had a dozen odd-man advantages, but while the Oilers converted on three of their chances they also limited the Kings to no goals while Los Angeles was on the power play. The teams exchanged even-strength goals in the first period, but less than two minutes into the second Chris Pronger wired

Los Angeles forward Joe Corvo tries to beat Ty Conklin to the far side, but the goalie gets his blocker arm on the shot and steers the puck out of harm's way.

a shot past Mathieu Garon with the extra man to give the Oilers the lead. One penalty after another ensued, but during brief 5-on-5 play Los Angeles managed two goals to pull ahead 3–2. The Oilers, as had become their custom, pulled away in the third, though. They outshot the Kings 18–8 and scored the only three goals of the period to claim the two points. Raffi Torres tied the game midway through the period and Ales Hemsky had a Pronger slapshot bounce off his foot and behind Garon on a power play to give Edmonton a 4–3 lead. This proved to be the game winner as Michael Peca added a goal into the empty net while Los Angeles was playing short-handed but with Garon on the bench to make it five skaters a side. Technically, though, it was still called a power-play goal.

Oilers' defenceman Chris Pronger gets in the way of Wild star Marian Gaborik on this play, but Gaborik scored twice to lead his team to a 4–2 win in Edmonton.

December 26, 2005
Minnesota 4 at Edmonton 1

A double-home, two-game series against Minnesota to start the post-Christmas season went awry for Edmonton, thanks in part to some spotty goaltending from Ty Conklin, in part to a lack of energy by his teammates in front of him. The Oilers' five-game winning streak came to a grinding halt either way. Fernando Pisani scored the game's only goal of the first period to stake the home side to a 1–0 lead, but that was to be the only positive this night for Edmonton. Pascal Dupuis tied the game in the second on a Wild power play, but the backbreaker was Marian Gaborik's go-ahead goal with just 45

seconds left in the second period. Minnesota pulled away in the third as the Oilers could not beat Manny Fernandez in the Wild net. Coupled with Calgary's win, the Oilers and Flames were now tied for first place in the division.

December 28, 2005
Minnesota 4 at Edmonton 2

For the second straight game the Oilers let down their home fans with a sub-par effort. This was especially frustrating because they dominated the first period yet trailed 2–0 after 20 minutes. Although they outshot Minnesota, 9–4, the Wild scored on their first two shots and Ty Conklin

had his second straight shaky outing, suggesting again the Oilers needed more reliable goaltending if they were to qualify for the playoffs. When Brian Rolston scored on the power play early in the second, the fans sensed the game was pretty much over and there would be no rallies that characterized the team's wins prior to Christmas. The Oilers tried, though. Steve Staios made it 3–1 before the end of the second, and Ales Hemsky scored a minute into the third to draw within a goal. The stifling Minnesota team defence didn't allow the Oilers much offense, though, and a penalty-free third ended with an empty-net goal from Gaborik to finish the scoring.

December 30, 2005
Nashville 2 at **Edmonton 4**

Happy to shake the claustrophobic play of Minnesota, the Oilers greeted visiting Nashville with a more wide-open game and came away victors as a result. Ryan Smyth scored the eventual game winner on a penalty shot early in the third, beating Tomas Vokoun with a nice move to make the score 3–1 at that point. A goalless first period gave way to three scores in the second, Edmonton getting the first and last with a Scott Hartnell goal for the Predators in between. Shawn Horcoff and Jason Smith were given credit for those goals. Steve Sullivan made it 3–2 after Smyth's free shot had given the Oilers a two-goal lead, and Jarret Stoll rounded out the scoring with a late goal to make it 4–2. Jussi Markkanen stopped 29 of 31 Nashville shots. The win put the Oilers back into a tie for first place in the division with idle Calgary, though the Flames had a game in hand. Edmonton went just 1–8 with the power play.

December 31, 2005
Edmonton 5 at **Calgary 6**

A game to decide the outright lead in the Northwest Division went to the hometown Flames as Calgary ended 2005 as leaders. The deciding goal was scored late and lucky, but a win is a win and the Flames weren't about to complain. Kristian Huselius got a goal with just 1:15 left in regulation time. Captain Jarome Iginla won a faceoff deep in the Edmonton end, and Huselius took the puck and fired a quick wrist shot through a maze of players in front. The puck hit two sets of legs along the way and pinballed past a stunned Jussi Markkanen who had no chance to stop a puck he couldn't see. It was a see-saw game that started with Calgary going up 2–0 midway through the first period.

Goalie Jussi Markkanen keeps his eye on the puck even as Nashville's Vernon Fiddler is right on top of him.

Raffi Torres and Marc-Andre Bergeron tied the game, however, and midway through the second Jarret Stoll put the Oilers up 3–2 with a power-play score. Matt Lombardi scored late to tie the game and then Sean Donovan scored only 18 seconds into the third to give the Flames another lead. Ryan Smyth scored his team-best 17th goal to tie the game at 4–4, and the teams exchanged goals to make it 5–5 with time winding down. That set the stage for Huselius's crazy game winner, giving Calgary 50 points to Edmonton's 48.

Ryan Smyth tries to stuff the puck in the short side but Toronto goalie Mikael Tellqvist gets his pad over to the post in time to make the save.

January 3, 2006
Chicago 0 at **Edmonton 5**

The Oilers rang in 2006 by recording their first shutout of the season, and despite their woeful record it was also the first shutout loss by the Hawks who had won only 13 of their 39 games to date. Ty Conklin stopped all 23 Hawks shots for the win, and Edmonton scored in every period. Shawn Horcoff put the Oilers on the board 2:47 into the first period off a nice pass from Ales Hemsky, but it was the second period that defined the game. Edmonton scored three times in the middle 20 minutes to take control and then coasted in the third, Jani Rita adding a late and meaningless goal to finish the scoring. Edmonton did not draw a penalty in the final 40 minutes of the game. Ryan Smyth scored his team leading 18th goal and Horcoff's goal gave him 41 points, tops of the team. Ales Hemsky, second with 39 points, assisted on Horcoff's goal in the first.

January 7, 2006
Toronto 3 at Edmonton 2

As always when the Leafs travel the country, there were more Toronto fans than Oilers fans at Rexall Place, giving the building a charged atmosphere long before the opening faceoff. The Leafs didn't help the Edmonton cause on this western trip, first losing to Calgary the previous night 1–0 and then defeating the Oilers this night to push the Oilers further behind the Flames for the division lead. Ty Conklin looked a bit weak on Toronto's first two goals in the first which gave the visitors some life after the opening period. Shawn Horcoff scored the only goal of the second at 19:37, but rather than wilt to start the third the Leafs came out strong and fresh and went ahead 3–1 thanks to some great work by Chad Kilger who knocked home a rebound for his goal. Ryan Smyth bounced a shot off goalie Mikael Tellqvist midway through the third to make it 3–2, but the

Leafs weathered the Edmonton attack the rest of the way and held on. The Oilers had a chance to tie after Alexander Khavanov took a late tripping penalty, but Tellqvist stood tall in the Leafs net and the Blue and White left Alberta with a win and a loss.

January 10, 2006
Edmonton 3 at Pittsburgh 1

The Oilers were seeing 18-year-old sensation Sidney Crosby for the first time, but Sid the Kid was not a factor in this game. Shawn Horcoff was. He scored all three Oilers goals—one at even strength, one on the power play, and one short-handed. The Penguins got their only goal in the third when Ryan Malone tipped a Josef Melichar shot past Jussi Markkanen. The Oilers have never shut out the Penguins since joining the NHL in 1979. Horcoff's short hander was the only goal of the first—a shot that

Edmonton forward Michael Peca keeps his body between Pittsburgh rookie sensation Sidney Crosby and the goal.

beat Marc-Andre Fleury five-hole— but despite a huge edge in play a goalless second produced a close game for the final period thanks to the goaltending of Fleury in the Penguins net. Horcoff scored 44 seconds into that final period on a backhand from in tight to give the Oilers a bit of breathing room, and he finished his hat trick night with a last-minute goal on the power play. Pittsburgh's record dropped to a dismal 11–22–9. Only St. Louis had fewer wins (10). Edmonton outshot Pittsburgh 31–18.

January 12, 2006
Edmonton 4 at **NY Rangers 5** (OT)

A back-and-forth game ended badly for Edmonton when the league's leading scorer, Jaromir Jagr, notched his 28th goal of the season on a quick snapshot just 14 seconds into overtime to lift the Rangers to a home win over the Oilers. The game was preceded by a lengthy (75 minutes) tribute to Mark Messier, who retired prior to the season, climaxing with his number 11 being raised to the rafters of Madison Square Garden. Feeding off this emotion, the Rangers jumped into the early lead, scoring the only goal of the first. The Oilers had the

better of play, though, and they made it count in the second when they reeled off three straight goals through the first half of the period. Michael Peca, Ales Hemsky, and Marc-Andre Bergeron gave the Oilers a handsome 3–1 lead, but two late goals by the Blueshirts evened the score before the second intermission. Petr Prucha gave the Rangers a lead, and Peca, with his second of the night, tied the game midway through the third to send the game into overtime. The Oilers first had to kill a late penalty to Todd Harvey, one of ten power plays they gave the Rangers (allowing one goal). Jagr's was the only shot of the OT, but it was all that was needed.

Ryan Smyth, stationed perfectly in front of Dominik Hasek, tips the puck past the goalie for a second-period goal.

January 14, 2006
Ottawa 5 at Edmonton 3

A second-period collapse turned a 2–1 lead into a 4–2 deficit for the Oilers as they suffered their second straight loss. This came at the expense of Ottawa which, with the win, moved up into a tie for first place overall in the NHL standings. Marc-Andre Bergeron had a hand in all Oilers goals, scoring twice and assisting on Ryan Smyth's 20th of the year, a deflection in the second period. Vaclav Varada put the Senators up early in the first but a pair of scores from Bergeron gave the hometown Oilers the lead after a period. His first score was a great slapshot from the point that beat Dominik Hasek. Ottawa blew the game open in the second, scoring three in a row and controlling the play for long stretches of 5-on-5.

Dany Heatley tied the game a minute into the period, and midway through Antoine Vermette and Peter Schaefer struck the death blow to the Oilers. As had happened frequently this season, a flurry of goals like this prompted coach Craig MacTavish to make a goaltending change. In this instance, Ty Conklin came out and Jussi Markkanen went in, but the move had little effect on the game's outcome. Vaclav Varada scored the only goal of the third to make it 5–3.

January 16, 2006
Buffalo 3 at Edmonton 1

The Oilers remained mired in fourth place in the Northwest Division after their third straight loss to make their record 24–17–5. Like so many games this season, the result might have been different but for more effective special teams. Buffalo scored two of their three goals on the power play—the Sabres had eleven man-advantage opportunities on the night—while the Oilers went goalless in five tries with the extra man. Ales Hemsky scored the game's first goal at 3:35, but Tim Connolly got it back late in the period with both Jason Smith and Shawn Horcoff in the penalty box. A scoreless second period saw the Oilers have three power plays and the Sabres six, the last of those a double minor to Jarret Stoll that carried over into the third. Early in the final period Maxim Afinogenov cashed in on that power play to give the Sabres a 2–1 lead, and later in the period he assisted on Derek Roy's goal that put the game out of reach. Jussi Markkanen played the whole game for Edmonton while Ryan Miller stopped 22 of 23 shots in the Buffalo net.

the extra point via the shootout. Morrison increased his part-time record to 6–1–0 while Vesa Toskala was in goal for the Sharks. The win improved Edmonton's road record to 14–8–3, better than their 11–9–2 record at Rexall Place.

January 21, 2006
Edmonton 3 at Phoenix 4 (SO)

It was a game the Oilers could have just as easily won as lost, but in the end the score was probably a fair result. For the second consecutive game they went to a shootout, but this time Phoenix got the upper hand as Jussi Markkanen was outduelled in the net by Curtis Joseph. Both Edmonton's Michael Peca and former Oilers Mike Comrie missed on the first shots, but the next two skaters both scored, Ryan Smyth with a wrist shot for the Oilers and Geoff Sanderson on the deke for Phoenix. The game boiled down to one shot each way, and after Joseph watched Ales Hemsky shoot wide at one end, Ladislav Nagy buried his shot to give the Coyotes the win. Both teams scored in the first period, but Mike Johnson's 12th of the year gave Phoenix a 2–1 lead after two periods. The Oilers responded in the third by scoring twice to take a 3–2 lead, but they, too, couldn't hold the opposition at bay. Oleg Saprykin scored at 16:19 off a rebound to send the game into overtime, but both teams must have been kicking themselves after the game because of obstruction penalties that killed the flow and their respective horrible power-play puck movement. Both the Oilers and Coyotes were 0–9 with the extra man. One good shift with the man advantage might well have given either team victory in regulation.

Edmonton's Marc-Andre Bergeron (left) fights for the puck against Buffalo's Derek Roy in the third period.

January 19, 2006
Edmonton 3 at San Jose 2 (SO)

A game that started out looking like an Edmonton win ended up looking like an Edmonton loss until Michael Peca and Ryan Smyth scored in the shootout to give the Oilers their first win since January 10. The Oilers went up 2–0 in the first period on goals by Shawn Horcoff and Steve Staios, but San Jose remained patient and chipped away at the Oilers' defence. Joe Thornton made it 2–1 in the second on a screen shot on the power play, and the Sharks tied the game in the third on a Milan Michalek goal at 8:05. In the overtime, Peca drew a penalty which the Oilers killed successfully, and in the shootout he made amends by scoring on the first shot. Nils Ekman, Thornton, and Patrick Marleau were all stopped by Mike Morrison to give the Oilers

January 23, 2006
Calgary 3 at Edmonton 1

Edmonton was the better team in every department except one, goaltending, and that was all the Flames needed to take two points from the game and put further space between themselves and the Oilers in the standings. The win was Calgary's fourth in a row and gave them 63 points, first in the division, while the Oilers remained in fourth with 56 points after losing their fourth in a row at home. Despite controlling the play in the first period, Edmonton went to the dressing room after 20 minutes trailing 1–0 courtesy of a Jarome Iginla goal, his 22nd on the year. Ales Hemsky tied the score for Edmonton at 8:41 of the second, but before the team could find its footing Kristian Huselius put the Flames back on top. That goal came just 16 seconds after Hemsky's, and Iginla added his second of the game a short time later. He thought he had a hat-trick goal in the third but it was ruled knocked in with a glove. Calgary goalie Miikka Kiprusoff was at his best in the third period when the Flames sat on the lead and the Oilers charged the goal only to be foiled time and again by the Finnish puckstopper. Mike Morrison lost for just the second time this year to go with six wins.

January 25, 2006
Edmonton 6 at Anaheim 3

Goaltending was the difference tonight as well, but this time it was the calm of Jussi Markkanen that prevailed over the frustrated and unnerved antics of Jean-Sebastien Giguere in the Anaheim net. Anaheim blew leads of 2–0 and 3–1, and the Oilers stole two points in a game they really should have lost. Teemu Selanne scored his 21st goal of the year early in the second period on the power play to give the Ducks

Anaheim goalie Jean-Sebastien Giguere loses his cool during the third period of Edmonton's win fuelled by power-play goals resulting from the goalie's meltdown.

a 2–0 edge, and he scored again a few minutes later after Marc-Andre Bergeron had replied for the Oilers. The visitors got their first big break when Steve Staios scored with less than two seconds left on the clock in the second period after a lazy save by Giguere that allowed a big rebound to come to Staios. Buoyed by that ending, the Oilers came out guns-a-blazin' in the third. A meltdown by Anaheim only helped the Oilers claim two points. It all began when Ales Hemsky scored at 3:42 to tie the game with a great shot over Giguere's glove. A few minutes later, Vitali Vishnevsky received a five-minute boarding major and game misconduct. During that extended power play, the Ducks took two more minor penalties to turn the long 5-on-4 into a long 5-on-3. First, Scott Niedermayer was sent off for cross-checking, and then Giguere was given a roughing penalty. Just 32 seconds later, the goalie was assessed a double minor and misconduct, putting his team down two men for another three and a half minutes. Through it all, Chris

Pronger scored two goals to put the Oilers up 5–3. They added another into an empty net.

January 26, 2006
Edmonton 5 at Los Angeles 3

The Oilers continued their western U.S. swing with another third-period rally to beat Los Angeles in a tamer game than what they had played the previous night. Ryan Smyth got the team off on the right foot with a power-play goal in the first minute, and that score held up until midway through the second when Luc Robitaille tied the game for the Kings courtesy of a superb, behind-the-back pass from Derek Armstrong. The teams exchanged goals later in the period to head to the dressing room 2–2 after 40 minutes, but it was the Oilers that pulled away in the third, scoring three times to the Kings' once. Raffi Torres scored early in the period off a nice pass from Georges Laraque behind the Kings' net, but the backbreaker was a short-handed effort from Ethan

Radek Dvorak gets high-fives from the bench after scoring what would be the game-winning goal during the shootout.

Moreau less than two minutes later when he beat Mathieu Garon with teammate Marty Reasoner in the box for hooking. It was Moreau's first goal in 18 games. Mike Morrison improved his record to 7–2–0. The Oilers improved their record to 27–18–6 and trailed the Flames atop the division by just three points again.

January 29, 2006
Edmonton 4 at Phoenix 3 (SO)

Finishing off a perfect three-game road trip, the Oilers beat Wayne Gretzky's Coyotes in a shootout that was extended to the third round of shots. Radek Dvorak finally made the difference, beating Curtis Joseph and then watching Mike Johnson stopped by Mike Morrison in the Edmonton goal. Earlier in the shootout, Ales Hemsky had scored for the Oilers and Shane Doan for Phoenix to send the shootout to sudden death. The game itself saw the lead swing back and forth. As had been the case all year, a successful power play would have made all the difference in the world. Tonight, the Oilers went goalless in eight tries while giving up one goal on eight Phoenix man-advantage chances. Zbynek Michalek gave Phoenix the lead after the first period, and then goals by Raffi Torres and Ryan Smyth put the Oilers in the lead. No sooner had Edmonton established that lead, though, than Phoenix struck back with two late goals to head to the dressing room ahead again. The Oilers were relentless in the third as the Coyotes held on for dear life, and they fell just one second short of escaping with a 3–2 win. Chris Pronger tied the game with Morrison on the bench and less than a second left on the clock. After an overtime which produced just one shot (that credited to the Coyotes), the Oilers pulled out the win in a shootout.

Jason Chimera beats Jussi Markkanen with a move to the forehand to give Columbus a win in the shootout.

February 2, 2006
Columbus 2 at Edmonton 1 (SO)

A second consecutive shootout game produced a loss for the Oilers, but it was a wild series of penalty shots nonetheless that ended this tense game. For the Blue Jackets, this was their fifth win in a row. A tentative and listless first period led to a big Oilers second period, but the game remained scoreless after 40 minutes thanks to the fine work in the Columbus goal by Marc Denis. Steve Staios looked to have scored the winning goal at 14:52 of the third period, but the Oilers couldn't hang on for the win. Nikolai Zherdev tied the game just two minutes later, and the overtime produced few chances and no goals. The shootout was all that the league promised it would be when the tie-breaking format was introduced at the start of the season. Jaroslav Balastik and Ales Hemsky scored for their respective teams to start the show, and the next four shooters all missed. Zherdev scored on his shot, forcing Fernando Pisani to score and continue the shootout or miss and lose the game for Edmonton. Pisani came through in style, and the penalty shots continued. Four more shooters failed to light the lamp, but Trevor Letowksi again put the pressure on the Oilers by scoring. Jarret Stoll responded by beating Denis, but in the next round Jason Chimera converted a fourth time for Columbus in the shootout and Shawn Horcoff could not answer back for the Oilers.

February 4, 2006
Vancouver 1 at **Edmonton 3**

Making a case to be the number-one goalie, backup Mike Morrison put in another good game and backstopped the Oilers to an impressive victory over the Canucks. It was the fifth straight win for the Oilers over their rivals from British Columbia, and the two points put Edmonton just two behind both Vancouver and Calgary for top spot in the division. Morrison, meanwhile, improved his record to 9–2–0. The score was closer than the game as the Oilers outshot Vancouver 40–17 and played more disciplined hockey as well. Edmonton built a 2–0 lead courtesy of goals from Ryan Smyth (his 23rd) and Jarret Stoll (his first since New Year's Eve), and Daniel Sedin made things a bit interesting when he closed the gap with a goal late in the second period. The Canucks could not take momentum from this score, however, and in the third period they were outshot 15–1 by a more aggressive Oilers team. Raffi Torres put the final nail in the coffin when he scored on a power play, Todd Bertuzzi in the box for tripping.

February 6, 2006
Anaheim 5 at **Edmonton 6** (SO)

Claiming their fourth win in five games, the Oilers were playing like a team trying to finish high in the standings instead of one just hoping to squeak into the playoffs. This was another win over Anaheim, but unlike the previous game Ducks goalie J-S Giguere was superb and kept the score close. Mike Morrison stopped all three Anaheim shots in the shootout to improve his record to a perfect 5–0 in the penalty-shot competition, and Fernando Pisani scored the only goal to give his team the win. The Oilers jumped into a quick 2–0 lead only to see that lead vanish

Fernando Pisani makes a great move before sliding the puck between the pads of J-S Giguere to win the shootout for the Oilers.

before the first intermission. Ryan Smyth and Marc-Andre Bergeron got the goals for the Oilers while Andy McDonald and Corey Perry replied for the Ducks. In the second, the teams exchanged goals, and early in the third they swapped markers again. Jaroslav Spacek scored at 4:28, but just 43 seconds later Todd Marchant tied the game. Two minutes after that the Ducks went ahead on a Scott Niedermayer score, a goal that convinced coach Craig MacTavish to switch goalies. Jussi Markkanen went to the bench, and Morrison went into the game. Pisani rounded out the regulation scoring with a goal at 10:27 and then redoubled his heroics in the shootout.

February 7, 2006
Edmonton 2 at **Colorado 5**

Playing their fourth game in six nights, the Oilers showed signs of fatigue in their lacklustre loss to Colorado. They had played late the previous night before hopping on a plane to Denver to play a mile above sea level, a fact that didn't help their cause. Nevertheless, all teams had this sort of schedule, especially in the compressed Olympic season which was fast approaching its climax. Players would head to Torino, Italy, in a week's time, and many were thinking about Olympic hockey as much as NHL hockey these days. The first period was a quiet affair, but Colorado scored three of the four goals in the second period to take the Oilers out of the game. Jarret Stoll scored for Edmonton on a one-timer off an Ales Hemsky pass on the power play, but Rob Blake's goal at 19:47 sent the Avs to the dressing room up 3–1. Radek Dvorak made it close early in the third, but Colorado came right back with two more quick strikes to cruise to victory. Mike Morrison suffered just his third loss of the year, but his team was outshot by a wide margin, 35–18. Both teams scored twice on the power play. For the Avs, it was welcome relief after going 0–15 with the man advantage in their previous two games.

Raffi Torres makes a nice move in close to beat goalie Dwayne Roloson.
Soon, the two would be teammates in Edmonton.

St. Louis 5 at Edmonton 4 (SO)

The Oilers wobbled to the Olympic break with their third straight loss, this via the shootout to St. Louis which had only 16 wins on the year, second lowest in the NHL behind Pittsburgh (14). Dennis Wideman was the hero for the Blues, scoring the only goal of the six shootout shots. In an attempt to strategize for the shootout, coach Craig MacTavish inserted goalie Mike Morrison for the shootout because of his 5–0 record even though Morrison was pulled in the first period after allowing two goals on the first five shots he faced. It was not Morrison's night, though, as he suffered his first shootout loss. Curtis Sanford stopped all three Edmonton shooters. Edmonton twice held the lead in the first period and twice allowed the Blues to tie the game. Lee Stempniak scored the only goal of the second to give St. Louis a 3–2 lead, but Ryan Smyth tied the game early in the third with his 27th goal of the season, tops on the team. Two late goals sent the game into overtime. Jay McClement may have though his goal at 16:24 would be enough for St. Louis, but Georges Laraque scored for Edmonton, just his second of the season, at 17:37. The overtime was highly entertaining with several fine scoring chances but, ultimately, no goals. Ales Hemsky, Smyth, and Pisani all missed for Edmonton in the shootout. The Oilers headed to the Olympic break with a fine 30–20–8 record, and although they were only in fourth place in their division, they were also just five points back of Calgary for first.

February 10, 2006
Minnesota 6 at Edmonton 3

The Oilers were never in this game and continued to have troubles against Minnesota, this time falling behind 3–0 in a one-sided first period made worse by a sub-par performance from goalie Mike Morrison. Marc Chouinard scored the first goal when he batted in a loose puck, video replay confirming his stick was below the crossbar when he made contact. Pierre-Marc Bouchard scored twice in a 16 second-span late in the first to spot the Wild to a lead that proved insurmountable. The Oilers got close in the second when Raffi Torres and Radek Dvorak scored, but Minnesota pulled ahead with two more before the end of the second. Morrison was pulled in favour of Ty Conklin to start the third, and he stopped all nine shots he faced. The Wild scored into the empty net after Todd Harvey had made it 5–3. Minnesota scored twice in nine power plays while the Oilers continued their season-long struggle with the extra man, failing to score on nine chances of their own, including a 5-on-3 in the third.

2006 Olympic Winter Games Torino

Name	Country	GP	G	A	P	Pim	Placing
Oilers' Participation							
Ales Hemsky	CZE	8	1	2	3	2	3rd
Chris Pronger	CAN	6	1	2	3	16	7th
Ryan Smyth	CAN	6	0	1	1	4	7th
Jaroslav Spacek	CZE	8	0	1	1	2	3rd

Canada's Ryan Smyth tries a wraparound as Italy's goalie Jason Muzzatti blocks his way.

2006 Olympics Results

Preliminary Round

Group A

Group A	GP	W	L	T	GF	GA	P
Finland	5	5	0	0	19	2	10
Switzerland	5	2	1	2	10	12	6
Canada	5	3	2	0	15	9	6
Czech Republic	5	2	3	0	14	12	4
Germany	5	0	3	2	7	16	2
Italy	5	0	3	2	9	23	2

Date	Team	Score	Team	Score
February 15	Canada	7	Italy	2
	Finland	5	Switzerland	0
	Czech Republic	4	Germany	1
February 16	Canada	5	Germany	1
	Finland	6	Italy	0
	Switzerland	3	Czech Republic	2
February 18	Switzerland	2	Canada	0
	Germany	3	Italy	3
	Finland	4	Czech Republic	2
February 19	Finland	2	Canada	0
	Germany	2	Switzerland	2
	Czech Republic	4	Italy	1
February 21	Canada	3	Czech Republic	2
	Switzerland	3	Italy	3
	Finland	2	Germany	0

Group B

Group B	GP	W	L	T	GF	GA	P
Slovakia	5	5	0	0	18	8	10
Russia	5	4	1	0	23	11	8
Sweden	5	3	2	0	15	12	6
USA	5	1	3	1	13	13	3
Kazakhstan	5	1	4	0	9	16	2
Latvia	5	0	4	1	11	29	1

Date	Team	Score	Team	Score
February 15	Sweden	7	Kazakhstan	2
	Slovakia	5	Russia	3
	Latvia	3	USA	3
February 16	Russia	5	Sweden	0
	Slovakia	6	Latvia	3
	USA	4	Kazakhstan	1
February 18	Russia	1	Kazakhstan	0
	Sweden	6	Latvia	1
	Slovakia	2	Kazakhstan	1
February 19	Russia	9	Latvia	2
	Slovakia	2	Kazakhstan	1
	Sweden	2	USA	1
February 21	Kazakhstan	5	Latvia	2
	Slovakia	3	Sweden	0
	Russia	5	USA	4

*Jaroslav Spacek of the Czech Republic (left) celebrates his team's bronze medal at Torino
with teammates Jaromir Jagr (centre) and Martin Rucinsky (right).*

Playoffs

Quarter-finals	February 22	Russia 2	Canada 0
		Sweden 6	Switzerland 2
		Finland 4	USA 3
		Czech Republic 3	Slovakia 1
Semi-finals	February 24	Finland 4	Russia 0
		Sweden 7	Czech Republic 2
Bronze Medal Game	February 25	Czech Republic 3	Russia 0
Gold Medal Game	February 26	Sweden 3	Finland 2

Shawn Horcoff celebrates his tying goal early in the third period. The Oilers scored once more to win, 3–2.

March 1, 2006
St. Louis 4 at Edmonton 2

The Oilers ended their pre-Olympic schedule with a loss to St. Louis and started the stretch run to the playoffs after Torino 2006 with another loss to the Blues, this time 4–2. They deserved a better fate this night, though, outshooting St. Louis by a three-to-one ratio (37–12), yet the Blues scored on one-third of their shots. Jussi Markkanen was less than excellent in goal for Edmonton as coach Craig MacTavish was having an awful time trying to find a number-one man. Not Markkanen, Mike Morrison, or Ty Conklin played well enough for long enough to suggest he was the man, so the coach was forever rotating his goalies in the hopes one would get hot and take charge of the crease. Tonight, Markkanen was yanked after two periods in favour of Morrison, but by that time the damage had been done. St. Louis led 2–0 after the first and added a third goal late in the second period. A Chris Pronger power-play goal on a slapshot got the Oilers back into it at 18:38 of the second and Marc-Andre Bergeron made it 3–2 early in the third. That was as close as the Oilers came. Scott Young added an insurance goal late to send the Rexall Place fans home disappointed. Yan Stastny made his debut for the Oilers.

March 3, 2006
San Jose 2 at Edmonton 3

A game that started out lethargically ended with a bang thanks to a great goal by Ales Hemsky with just 1:07 left in the third period. Hemsky beat San Jose defenceman Josh Gorges one-on-one with a beautiful move

A penalty shot or shootout shot, it makes no difference to Jussi Jokinen. Here he converts a penalty shot in the second period, beating Ty Conklin.

and then tucked the puck past goalie Vesa Toskala to score the winning goal in dramatic fashion. It capped a third period in which all five goals were scored. Both teams had their chances in the first 40 minutes but goalies Toskala and Ty Conklin were perfect. The Oilers opened the scoring 3:29 into the third when Raffi Torres won a battle for the puck in front of Toskala, but the Sharks came right back to tie on a Patrick Marleau score just 17 seconds later. The visitors got the upper hand late in the game, at 15:23, but Edmonton rallied to score twice before the game ended. Shawn Horcoff tied the game with his 17th goal of the season, and then Hemsky won the game for the Oilers with just over a minute to play. The pre-game ceremonies featured Hayley Wickenheiser, recently-returned captain of Canada's gold-medal women's team from Torino.

March 5, 2006
Nashville 2 at **Edmonton 3** (OT)

The Oilers' anemic power play finally came to life in a big way tonight, scoring three times on eleven opportunities including a goal at 4:17 of overtime to give the team a victory. Chris Pronger's slapshot from the point beat goalie Tomas Vokoun in the final minute of the extra period with Ryan Suter in the penalty box for hooking. Nashville scored two of the three goals in the first period, Ryan Smyth's 28th of the season sandwiched in between Predators goals from Scottie Upshall and Paul Kariya. There was no scoring in the second, but in the third Pronger began his heroics when another slapshot beat Vokoun from the point with the man advantage to tie the game. In overtime, Pronger replicated his efforts to give the

Oilers their second straight win. On both shots, Ryan Smyth provided an effective screen in front of Vokoun. The two points also gave the team a four-point gap over Anaheim in the battle for eighth place in the conference, the final playoff spot.

March 7, 2006
Dallas 4 at Edmonton 3 (SO)

The remarkable shootout juggernaut that was the Dallas Stars could not be stopped by Edmonton this night, and the Oilers, who had mounted an impressive third-period comeback, fell just short of stealing two points. Defenceman Sergei Zubov and the amazing Jussi Jokinen scored for the Stars in the penalty shot contest while both Ales Hemsky and Ryan Smyth drew blanks for the Oilers. It was Jokinen's ninth straight shootout goal. Marty Turco was the winning goalie and Mike Morrison, making another appearance from the bullpen, as it were, lost for the second straight time after winning his first five shootouts. The game was tied 1–1 midway through the second period after a Philippe Boucher goal put the Stars ahead and Dick Tarnstrom replied for the Oilers. Antti Miettinen put Dallas ahead midway through the second and then Jokinen made it 3–1 on— what else?—a penalty shot. That set the stage for a great rally before the hometown fans in the third. Smyth made it 3–2 at 3:52 and then Shawn Horcoff tied the game at 10:57. Ty Conklin played the entire 65 minutes in net for Edmonton, but then coach Craig MacTavish decided to go with Morrison for the shootout. The strategy didn't work, and the Stars claimed the extra point.

Dwayne Roloson makes a routine save in his first game with the Oilers. He played every game but the last of the regular season for the Oilers.

March 9, 2006
Edmonton 2 at **San Jose 5**

Dwayne Roloson, the newly-acquired goalie from the Minnesota Wild, made his debut for the Oilers this night, but the party was spoiled by a determined San Jose Sharks team. The Sharks took a 2–2 game after 40 minutes and made it their own in the final period, scoring three unanswered goals to win the game handily. Joe Thornton scored the backbreaker just eleven seconds into the final period after taking a pass from linemate Jonathan Cheechoo. Steve Bernier scored the other two Sharks goals. The teams played a scoreless first before

San Jose got on the board thanks to Milan Michalek at 1:01 of the middle 20 minutes. Jarret Stoll tied the game, and after the Sharks went ahead again Raffi Torres managed to beat Vesa Toskala to make it 2–2. That was as close as the Oilers got, however, as the Sharks pulled away in the last period. Ales Hemsky and Shawn Horcoff, Edmonton's top two scorers, were both held pointless while Thornton's goal and assist moved him to 90 points, just two behind league leader Jaromir Jagr. The Oilers remained stalled in eighth place in the Western Conference overall standings, three points ahead of the Mighty Ducks.

March 11, 2006
Edmonton 3 at **Columbus 4** (OT)

It was the second game for goalie Dwayne Roloson and the first for Sergei Samsonov since being acquired from Boston, but this was a game the Oilers should have won and didn't. They blew leads of 2–0 and 3–1 and lost the game in overtime on a sloppy play. Rostislav Klesla scored the winner with 54 seconds left in the game on a bad-angle shot that Roloson should have stopped. The Oilers didn't register a single shot in the five-minute extra period. They jumped into a 2–0 lead in the first period on the strength of two power-play goals, the first from Ryan Smyth, his 30th of the year off a perfect pass from Samsonov, and the second from Jaroslav Spacek. Trevor Letowski brought the Blue Jackets to within one early in the second, but Michael Peca restored the two-goal lead and the Oilers seemed to be in control. That comfort level didn't last long, though, as Sergei Fedorov scored for Columbus before the end of the second. Nikolai Zherdev tied the game midway through the third, and the Oilers spent the last four minutes of the game killing off consecutive penalties, fortunate to get to overtime and earn a point.

March 12, 2006
Edmonton 3 at Minnesota 4

The Oilers lost for the fourth time in a row and their once solid grip on a playoff spot was now in serious jeopardy. The loss, coupled with an Anaheim win, actually put the Oilers in ninth place in the Western Conference, out of a playoff spot, and the Ducks snuck into eighth. Five of the seven goals were scored on the power play. Minnesota went 3–10 with the extra man and the Oilers scored twice on four chances. It was the third straight loss for the Oilers with new goalie Dwayne Roloson in the net. Roloson was playing against his old team this night, but it was the Wild and goalie Manny Fernandez who came out on top. The Oilers blew two leads again. They were up 2–1 in the first after trailing 1–0, getting goals from Shawn Horcoff and Sergei Samsonov who made a great deke before roofing a backhander over Fernandez. Fernando Pisani made it 3–2 early in the third, but the Wild scored two more times in the middle part of the period to gain the upper hand.

Oilers players watch the tense final minute of the third period as they try unsuccessfully to tie the game against Minnesota.

March 14, 2006
Edmonton 2 at Minnesota 1

Earlier in the year the Oilers and Wild played a double-home series in Edmonton (swept by the Wild), and this was the second of a similar two-game set in Minnesota. Edmonton finally won a game, this a narrow decision that it almost lost again. The win was the first for goalie Dwayne Roloson with his new team, and the two points vaulted the Oilers back into a tie for eighth place in the conference standings while relegating idle Anaheim down to ninth. The win also snapped a four-game winless streak on the road for the Oilers. Chris Pronger scored in the first period on a long slapshot. Goalie Manny Fernandez was screened on the play by his own defenceman. Ryan Smyth, on a power play, scored in the second when Fernandez lost sight of the puck in the crease after making the initial save and Smyth just poked the unclaimed puck over the red line. The third was a wild period which saw Minnesota fight back to within one on an early goal. Try as they might, they couldn't beat Roloson with the tying goal and the Oilers ended their road winless streak.

Raffi Torres is poke-checked by Miikka Kiprusoff in goal as superstar rookie Dion Phaneuf helps out.

March 16, 2006
Calgary 2 at **Edmonton 3** (OT)

Such was the precariousness of the conference standings that one day the Oilers were out of the playoffs and two days later they were solidly in sixth place closing in on fifth. That was the case after this huge win over provincial rivals Calgary for their second win in a row. Shawn Horcoff was the hero, backhanding a goal 3:04 into an overtime dominated by the Oilers. Calgary went scoreless on seven power-play opportunities,

and Dwayne Roloson stopped 18 of 20 shots for the victory. The teams exchanged first-period goals, Jaroslav Spacek counting for Edmonton and Matt Lombardi connecting a few minutes later for the visiting Flames. It was a routine shot Roloson normally would have stopped. Mike Leclerc scored the only goal of the second for Calgary, and it was only the fine play of Roloson that kept this a one-goal game after 40 minutes. In the third, the tide turned and the Oilers controlled play. They tied the game at 7:12 courtesy of Jarret Stoll,

and in the overtime it was newcomer Sergei Samsonov who made a great pass to Horcoff for the game winner.

March 18, 2006
Detroit 4 at Edmonton 3 (SO)

The Oilers gained a point in the standings but lost one on the strength of a shootout loss to the Red Wings. This was a game the Oilers felt like they had won, thanks largely to a short-handed goal with less than two minutes to go in regulation time by

Fernando Pisani to send the game to overtime. Henrik Zetterberg, the leading Detroit point getter with 72, opened the scoring in the first period on the power play, his 35th goal of the season. Jarret Stoll replied for Edmonton a short time later and midway through the second Steve Staios gave the Oilers a 2–1 lead. This time it was the Wings that replied quickly. In the third the teams exchanged goals again, Detroit's Tomas Holmstrom scoring first before Pisani connected with Stoll in the penalty box. Pisani made a great play to steal the puck in the Detroit end, and as he fell he fired a shot that beat the surprised Manny Legace in the Red Wings goal. In the shootout, Pavel Datsyuk for Detroit and Pisani missed their shots in the first round. Jason Williams then converted for Detroit and Samsonov missed for the Oilers. Zetterberg sealed the win by beating Dwayne Roloson to give the Wings an insurmountable 2–0 lead in shootout goals.

March 21, 2006
Vancouver 4 at Edmonton 1

The new NHL featured more division games and more mini-series, sometimes consecutive games in the same city against one opponent or sometimes, like this set, a three-game series against the same opponent. This win by the Canucks was critical because it vaulted Vancouver into a tie for seventh place in the Western Conference with Anaheim with 80 points and pushed the Oilers to the brink, in eighth with 79 points, the

Newly-acquired forward Sergei Samsonov hangs onto the crossbar after a collision that sent the net off its moorings.

same as Los Angeles, for the final playoff position. Vancouver started the game with a greater sense of urgency, much to the dismay of the Edmonton fans, outshooting the Oilers 17–9 and outscoring them 2–0. Trevor Linden and Daniel Sedin did the damage, and as it turned out that was enough. Edmonton took a series of bad penalties in the second period, five minors in all, which prevented the team from building on a Raffi Torres goal just 1:10 into that period which got the Oilers back in the game. Ryan Kesler scored a little later, and it was only the good play of Dwayne Roloson that the score wasn't higher. Overall, the Canucks scored just once on ten power-play chances, and the Oilers were naught for their five chances. Sedin added his second of the night late in the third period to finish the scoring, and the teams flew on to Vancouver where they would play again two nights later.

March 23, 2006
Edmonton 3 at **Vancouver 4** (SO)

The Oilers lost their third straight game, and second to Vancouver, in an exciting shootout before a packed house at GM Place. Todd Bertuzzi scored the winner to cap a wild game that both teams felt they should have (or, could have) won in regulation. Bertuzzi got the Canucks going in the first period, scoring the only goal midway through the opening 20 minutes. Henrik Sedin made it 2–0 early in the second, but this goal woke up the Oilers who realized the importance of the game in the standings. Most of the rest of the period was played in the Canucks end, and they put three pucks past Alex Auld to take the lead, 3–2. Raffi Torres scored his 24th of the season a few minutes after Sedin's goal, and he tied the game at 18:08 of the period. Just 48 seconds later, Fernando Pisani put the Oilers ahead, and they went to the dressing room full of optimism. The intermission gave the Canucks a chance to re-group, and both teams were tentative in the third. The Oilers killed off an early penalty to Torres, but Canucks captain Markus Naslund tied the game midway through the period to send the game to overtime. Little happened in the five minutes of 4-on-4, but the shootout was wild. Ales Hemsky missed the first shot for the Oilers and Naslund scored to make it 1–0. Ryan Smyth scored, but so did Jarkko Ruutu. Michael Peca tied the shootout 2–2, leaving the game in the hands of Bertuzzi. He beat Edmonton goalie Dwayne Roloson cleanly, and the Canucks celebrated a come-from-behind win after blowing a 2–0 lead.

Bingo! Ryan Smyth opens the scoring with this beautiful one-timer that goalie Alex Auld couldn't get over in time to stop.

March 25, 2006
Edmonton 3 at Vancouver 2

Edmonton's 71st game of the season was nothing short of critical. The Oilers had lost three in a row and allowed Vancouver to make up precious ground in the conference standings for the final playoff position, and a loss this night would have put Edmonton in ninth place, out of post-season play. With that in mind, the Oilers went out and played a complete game, hanging on for a 3–2 win that had the feel of a playoff game right from the opening faceoff. Ryan Smyth set the tone in the first period when he scored short-handed to give the Oilers a 1–0 lead. Ryan Kesler tied the game for Vancouver early in the second, but Sergei Samsonov restored the lead with a goal midway through the period on the power play. Steve Staios provided a two-goal margin early in the third, but the team didn't sit back and wait

for the final horn. The Oilers kept attacking, but Brendan Morrison's goal made it 3–2 and produced a nail-biting ending. When Samsonov took a cross-checking penalty at 18:35, the Canucks pulled goalie Alex Auld for a two-man advantage, but Dwayne Roloson and the defence preserved the big win for the Oilers. With the two points, they moved into a tie with the Canucks for seventh place in the conference standings, just one point up on ninth-place Los Angeles and two up on San Jose in tenth.

March 26, 2006
Edmonton 4 at Colorado 3 (SO)

While everyone looked at conference standings to see which eight teams would qualify for the playoffs, the Oilers were also looking at the division standings as well. In the former, the Oilers were just two points away from missing the

playoffs. In the latter, they were just two points out of first place which meant an automatic top-three placing in the conference standings. That's how close the race in the west continued to be as teams entered the final three weeks of the regular season. And so it was that this victory moved Edmonton into third place in the Northwest Division, just two points behind Calgary and this same Avalanche team, tied for first with 86 points. It was another huge win, this accomplished by the slimmest of margins in the shootout, newcomer Sergei Samsonov scoring the only goal on six total shots. Ryan Smyth scored the first goal of the game for the second straight night, a great one-timer on the power play, but Colorado struck back with two goals to take a 2–1 lead to the dressing room. Steve Staios tied the game in the final minute of the second period to set up a critical third period, and teams exchanged

Sergei Samsonov ties the game in the first period with this nice move on Wild goalie Manny Fernandez.

goals to send the game to overtime. Jarret Stoll scored first, his 20th of the season at 3:51 of the third for the Oilers, but Jim Dowd replied nine minutes later. The overtime was dominated by Colorado, but Dwayne Roloson outduelled Peter Budaj in the nets during the penalty-shot contest. Roloson stopped all three Avs players—Antti Laaksonen, Milan Hejduk, and Joe Sakic—fine scorers all.

March 28, 2006
Minnesota 3 at Edmonton 2

Colorado won, Calgary and San Jose lost, and Los Angeles didn't play. Those facts, coupled with the Oilers' loss, left Edmonton back in eighth spot in the conference by just two points yet also just two points out of fifth spot as well. The game saw the Oilers fail to hang on to another lead and play poorly against the Wild yet again as they kicked off a critical four-game homestand. After a goalless and penalty-free

first period, Minnesota got on the board first thanks to a Wes Walz short-handed score early in the second. The Oilers responded with two power-play goals late in the period to get their bearings, Sergei Samsonov and Jarret Stoll doing the damage. But in the third it was all Wild. They scored twice to turn a deficit into a lead and then played Minnesota-trap hockey, limiting the Oilers to just six shots. They had just four shots of their own and only 16 in the game, but Manny Fernandez stopped 23 of 25 Edmonton shots to claim the victory.

March 30, 2006
Los Angeles 0 at **Edmonton 4**

This was a true four-point game. Los Angeles was in tenth spot with 81 points while the Oilers were in eighth with 84. A Kings win would move them to within a single point of Edmonton; a loss would send them five back. In ninth spot was San Jose, and the Sharks did both

teams a favour by losing to Phoenix, 5–2. The Oilers took their cue from this and came out flying before the usual 16,839 home fans, and their two goals in the first propelled them to a key victory. Dwayne Roloson, making his 12th successive start since joining the Oilers, got his first shutout with his new team (and first since October 12, 2005), stopping all 20 Los Angeles shots. Raffi Torres made sure the crowd was a factor in the game by scoring after only 1:43 of play, and later in the period Sergei Samsonov scored on a play that started with Roloson playing the puck to defenceman Chris Pronger, and Pronger getting the puck to Samsonov. The Oilers poured it on in the second, adding two more goals from Jaroslav Spacek and Ales Hemsky. In the third, with enough goals to win, they shut the Kings down and cruised to victory. Hemsky had a goal and assist to give him 70 points, tied with Shawn Horcoff for the team lead.

Goalie Miikka Kiprusoff makes the glove save as Ethan Moreau looks for the rebound.

April 1, 2006
Calgary 4 at Edmonton 1

This was a battle in true Alberta tradition, and the Flames came away with the win after withstanding a fierce Edmonton start to the game. The result kept the Oilers stuck in eighth place, still just three very uncomfortable points up on both San Jose and Los Angeles for the final playoff spot. Despite taking it to the Flames to start the game, it was the Oilers that fell behind 1–0 after a Daymond Langkow goal. Radek Dvorak coughed the puck up deep in his end and Langkow beat Dwayne Roloson to deaden the Rexall Place crowd. The Flames pulled away early in the second period when Kristian Huselius scored two quick goals to make it 3–0, the first on a rebound, the second on a power play. Shawn Horcoff replied with one goal, but that was the only puck that beat Miikka Kiprusoff as he stopped the other 25 shots he faced. Brad Ference added

a power-play goal early in the third, and the Oilers were silenced the rest of the period.

April 3, 2006
Phoenix 1 at **Edmonton 7**

The margin of victory didn't matter as much as the two points tonight, as the Oilers won on a night all other teams bunched in the west won as well. Los Angeles, Colorado, and San Jose all were victorious, so although the Oilers collected two points with their impressive win over the Coyotes they didn't gain ground in the standings—they simply didn't lose ground. The Oilers broke the ice early in the game with two goals just 26 seconds apart, Shawn Horcoff scoring at 3:56 after Marc-Antoine Pouliot scored his first career goal to start the Oilers' evening when he controlled Brad Winchester's shot and made no mistake with the rebound. Mike Comrie gave the Coyotes life with a late goal, but the

second period was Oil and more Oil. Curtis Joseph surrendered four goals on just ten Edmonton shots, and by the second intermission it was a 6–1 game. Ethan Moreau, Marc-Andre Bergeron, Michael Peca, and Sergei Samsonov all scored to take the game out of reach. Coach Wayne Gretzky pulled Joseph in favour of rookie David LeNeveu to start the third, and the newcomer allowed just one goal on eleven shots. Phoenix controlled the period, but Edmonton did a good job staying out of the penalty box and Radek Dvorak scored the only goal of the final 20 minutes on a slapshot to make it a 7–1 final score.

April 6, 2006
Edmonton 1 at **Minnesota 2** (SO)

The Oilers picked up a valuable point in the standings, but they also lost one, too, after another loss to Minnesota. Coupled with San Jose's important 5–0 win over Los Angeles, the Oilers

Ryan Smyth makes a nice move to beat Nikolai Khabibulin in the first period.

and Sharks were now tied with 89 points for the final playoff spot while Vancouver was on the outside looking in, with 87 points. The Wild scored the only goal of the first period, but the turning point came early in the second. First, Ryan Smyth scored his 34th goal of the season while playing short-handed, Chris Pronger in the box for roughing. Soon after, though, Michael Peca thought he had scored a goal. The puck appeared to cross the goal line, but Manny Fernandez reached back and smothered the puck before the red light went on. Referees went to video review and upheld the no-goal call, but later it appeared from closer observation that the puck had, indeed, gone in. Regardless, the game remained tied 1–1 through the rest of the second period and all of the third, and the overtime produced no winner. In the shootout, Mikko Koivu and Sergei Samsonov exchanged goals on the

first shots. Then, Marian Gaborik and Ales Hemsky both missed. In the final round, Brian Rolston scored on Dwayne Roloson and Smyth was stopped by Fernandez, and the Wild skated off with two points.

April 7, 2006
Edmonton 4 at Chicago 3 (OT)

Nothing was guaranteed, of course, but for the first time in a long time the Oilers' playoff chances looked very good, indeed. With this huge overtime win, Ryan Smyth again coming through on the power play in the short, fourth period, the Oilers took sole possession of sixth spot in the conference with 91 points, one up on Colorado, two up on San Jose, and most important four up on Vancouver in ninth spot. It was a game that went from good to bad for Edmonton, though in the end the

two points was all that mattered. After swapping goals with the Hawks in the first period, the Oilers took a 3–1 lead in the second on scores from Ales Hemsky and Fernando Pisani, both power-play markers and the first coming in a 5-on-3 situation. They failed to hold the lead in the third, however, a nemesis that had cost them several points during the season. This time, it was a Kyle Calder goal at 18:01 that sent the game to overtime, but the Oilers' resolve was greater than their opponents'. They outshot Chicago 5–0 in the overtime, and early they thought they scored the winner when Pisani knocked the puck in past goalie Nikolai Khabibulin. Video review, for the second game in a row, denied the Oilers a goal, but they persisted and drew a penalty. With Patrick Sharp in the box for slashing, Smyth converted a pass from Hemsky to give the Oilers the win.

Ryan Smyth drives to the net and shoots wide as goalie Jason Bacashihua and defenceman Lee Stempniak team up to stop him.

April 9, 2006
Edmonton 1 at **St. Louis 2**

Controversy erupted even before the opening faceoff this night. The Blues, long eliminated from the playoffs and mired in a team-record 13-game losing streak, decided to honour Al MacInnis this night in a lengthy pre-game ceremony. MacInnis had retired at the beginning of the year, and St. Louis chose this night to retire his number 2. The Oilers, however, felt that a 45-minute honour prior to a game that was critical to their playoff fortunes was inappropriate at best, so they stayed in their dressing room while the Blues did MacInnis proud. If there were any gamesmanship to the ceremony, it worked, because the Oilers came out for the first period and played a flat, emotionless 20 minutes. In fact, they took four

minor penalties and were lucky to escape with a scoreless tie. They weren't so fortunate in the second, though, as Jamal Mayers scored in the first minute and goalie Jason Bacashihua stopped everything that came his way. The Oilers turned up the heat in the third, but Bacashihua was spectacular, stopping 22 of 23 shots he faced in that period alone. Yet it was the Blues that scored early in the third to go up 2–0, and Edmonton's power-play goal came at 19:35 when the game was all but over. Chris Pronger's shot beat Bacashihua, the former Blues' star having little to celebrate with a goal that spoiled the shutout but had little importance beside. The loss left the Oilers in eighth spot just a single point up on Vancouver, but the Canucks had a game in hand.

April 11, 2006
Edmonton 0 at **Detroit 2**

The Oilers weren't making things easy for themselves. This loss to the Red Wings, first in the NHL with 118 points, kept their playoff hopes perched on a most precarious cliff. Their main worry was the Vancouver Canucks, in ninth with 89 points and three games to play. Edmonton had 91 points but only two games left. Clearly one of these teams would make the playoffs at the other's expense. The win gave Detroit a lock on the Presidents' Trophy. Manny Legace stopped all 29 Oilers shots for the shutout, his seventh of the season. Minor-league veteran Don MacLean scored the first goal for Detroit midway through the first period with Michael Peca off for tripping, and a goalless second produced a desperate third period for Edmonton. Kris Draper scored just 19 seconds into the final 20 minutes, but the Oilers threw everything they could at Legace the rest of the way. He was brilliant in stopping 16 shots in the third, several of those excellent scoring chances that frustrated the Oilers. Edmonton went 0–5 on the power play at a time it desperately needed a goal, but the team headed toward its final games against conference opponents having lost the past two games.

April 13, 2006
Anaheim 1 at **Edmonton 2**

Vancouver lost its game the previous night, which represented the game in hand the Canucks had on Edmonton, and this night they lost again, 5–3 to San Jose. As a result, Edmonton's 2–1 win over Anaheim secured the Oilers a place in the playoffs—with just one game left in the season. And the win came in most dramatic fashion, Ales Hemsky scoring the go-ahead and winning goal with a mere 34 seconds left in the third period. Both teams scored in the first period, Edmonton opening the period with a goal three minutes in from Ethan Moreau, the Ducks coming back with their own score later in the period. Andy McDonald, one of the league's unsung stars, notched his 32nd of the year to tie the game, 1–1. The second period was tentatively played by both teams, and in the third, the Oilers aware of their playoff status, poured it on. Although they had to wait until the final minute to get the game winner, it was a just result based on their superior performance this night. On the goal, Hemsky took a quick shot inside the faceoff circle to J-S Giguere's glove side. The puck squirted between his pads and into the goal, sending the sold out Rexall

Raffi Torres tries to get a shot on goal as Jose Theodore follows the puck and defenceman Karlis Skrastins clears Torres out of the way.

Place crowd into cheers of delirium. Dwayne Roloson, starting in his 19th consecutive game for the Oilers, stopped 23 of 24 shots for the win.

April 17, 2006
Colorado 2 at **Edmonton 4**

With four days off between their 81st and 82nd games of the year, the Oilers were a well-rested team for their season finale against the Avalanche. They already knew they'd be playing the top-ranked Detroit Red Wings in the first round of the playoffs, so to that end coach Craig MacTavish rested seven regulars, notably goalie Dwayne Roloson who was missing his first game since coming to the team in a trade from Minnesota. Ty Conklin got the start, and he had to face only 17 shots from Colorado.

The Oilers got on the board first, on a goal by Rem Murray in the final minute of the opening period. Joe Sakic's 32nd of the season tied the game in the second, his 574th career goal which put him 17th on the all-time list. In the third, Raffi Torres scored early and Patrice Brisebois tied the game at 8:08. Jarret Stoll broke the game open when he got the go-ahead goal on a Colorado power play, beating Jose Theodore at 14:46. Jaroslav Spacek added an empty netter, and the Oilers finished their regular season in fine fashion. Their 41 wins and 95 points were best totals since 1987-88, a Stanley Cup year, when they won 44 times and had 99 points. This was the gratifying part, but ahead was the nightmare— a first-round playoff date with Detroit, a team loaded with stars and firing on all cylinders.

Edmonton Oilers
Player Statistics, 2005–06, Regular Season

	GP	G	A	P	Pim
Ales Hemsky	81	19	58	77	64
Shawn Horcoff	79	22	51	73	85
Jarret Stoll	82	22	46	68	74
Ryan Smyth	75	36	30	66	58
Chris Pronger	80	12	44	56	74
Raffi Torres	82	27	14	41	50
Fernando Pisani	80	18	19	37	42
Marc-Andre Bergeron	75	15	20	35	38
Steve Staios	82	8	20	28	84
Radek Dvorak	64	8	20	28	26
Ethan Moreau	74	11	16	27	87
Marty Reasoner	58	9	17	26	20
Michael Peca	71	9	14	23	56
Jaroslav Spacek	31	5	14	19	24
Jason Smith	76	4	13	17	84
Sergei Samsonov	19	5	11	16	6
Georges Laraque	72	2	10	12	73
Igor Ulanov	37	3	6	9	29
Todd Harvey	63	5	2	7	32
Cory Cross	34	2	3	5	38
Dick Tarnstrom	22	1	3	4	24
Jani Rita	21	3	0	3	6
Alexei Semenov	11	1	1	2	17
Rem Murray	9	1	1	2	2
Matt Greene	27	0	2	2	43
Marc-Antoine Pouliot	8	1	0	1	0
Brad Winchester	19	0	1	1	21
Dwayne Roloson	19	0	1	1	2
Mike Morrison	21	0	0	0	2
Jussi Markkanen	37	0	1	1	0
Dan Smith	7	0	0	0	7
Danny Syvret	10	0	0	0	6
Kyle Brodziak	10	0	0	0	4
Ty Conklin	18	0	0	0	2
Krys Kolanos	6	0	0	0	2
Jean-Francois Jacques	7	0	0	0	0
Yan Stastny	3	0	0	0	0
Mathieu Roy	1	0	0	0	0

Goalies

	GP	W-L-T	Mins	GA	SO	GAA
Dwayne Roloson	19	8-7-0	1,162	47	1	2.42
Ty Conklin	18	8-5-0	922	43	1	2.80
Mike Morrison	21	0-4-0	891	42	0	2.83
Jussi Markkanen	37	15-12-0	2,015	105	0	3.13

Final Standings,
Regular Season, 2005–06

WESTERN CONFERENCE
Northwest Division

	GP	W	L	OTL	SOL	GF	GA	P
Calgary Flames	82	46	25	4	7	218	200	103
Colorado Avalanche	82	43	30	3	6	283	257	95
Edmonton Oilers	82	41	28	4	9	256	251	95
Vancouver Canucks	82	42	32	4	4	256	255	92
Minnesota Wild	82	38	36	5	3	231	215	84

Central Division

	GP	W	L	OTL	SOL	GF	GA	P
Detroit Red Wings	82	58	16	5	3	305	209	124
Nashville Predators	82	49	25	5	3	259	227	106
Columbus Blue Jackets	82	35	43	1	3	223	279	74
Chicago Blackhawks	82	26	43	7	6	211	285	65
St. Louis Blues	82	21	46	6	9	197	292	57

Pacific Division

	GP	W	L	OTL	SOL	GF	GA	P
Dallas Stars	82	53	23	5	1	265	218	112
San Jose Sharks	82	44	27	4	7	266	242	99
Mighty Ducks of Anaheim	82	43	27	5	7	254	229	98
Los Angeles Kings	82	42	35	4	1	249	270	89
Phoenix Coyotes	82	38	39	2	3	246	271	81

EASTERN CONFERENCE
Northeast Division

	GP	W	L	OTL	SOL	GF	GA	P
Ottawa Senators	82	52	21	3	6	314	211	113
Buffalo Sabres	82	52	24	1	5	281	239	110
Montreal Canadiens	82	42	31	6	3	243	247	93
Toronto Maple Leafs	82	41	33	1	7	257	270	90
Boston Bruins	82	29	37	8	8	230	266	74

Atlantic Division

	GP	W	L	OTL	SOL	GF	GA	P
New Jersey Devils	82	46	27	5	4	242	229	101
Philadelphia Flyers	82	45	26	5	6	267	259	101
New York Rangers	82	44	26	8	4	257	215	100
New York Islanders	82	36	40	3	3	230	278	78
Pittsburgh Penguins	82	22	46	8	6	244	316	58

Southeast Division

	GP	W	L	OTL	SOL	GF	GA	P
Carolina Hurricanes	82	52	22	6	2	294	260	112
Tampa Bay Lightning	82	43	33	2	4	252	260	92
Atlanta Thrashers	82	41	33	3	5	281	275	90
Florida Panthers	82	37	34	6	5	240	257	85
Washington Capitals	82	29	41	6	6	237	306	70

(note: teams are awarded one point for an overtime loss (OTL) and a shootout loss (SOL))

2006 Playoff Results

Eastern Conference Quarter-finals

April 21 Tampa Bay 1 at Ottawa 4
April 23 Tampa Bay 4 at Ottawa 3
April 25 Ottawa 8 at Tampa Bay 4
April 27 Ottawa 5 at Tampa Bay 2
April 29 Tampa Bay 2 at Ottawa 3
Ottawa wins best-of-seven 4–1

April 22 Montreal 6 at Carolina 1
April 24 Montreal 6 at Carolina 5
        (Ryder 2:32 2OT)
April 26 Carolina 2 at Montreal 1
        (Staal 3:38 OT)
April 28 Carolina 3 at Montreal 2
April 30 Montreal 1 at Carolina 2
May 2 Carolina 2 at Montreal 1
        (Stillman 1:19 OT)
Carolina wins best of seven 4–2

April 22 NY Rangers 1 at New Jersey 6
April 24 NY Rangers 1 at New Jersey 4
April 26 New Jersey 3 at NY Rangers 0
        |Brodeur|
April 29 New Jersey 4 at NY Rangers 2
New Jersey wins best-of-seven 4–0

April 22 Philadelphia 2 at Buffalo 3
        (Briere 7:31 2OT)
April 24 Philadelphia 2 at Buffalo 8
April 26 Buffalo 2 at Philadelphia 4
April 28 Buffalo 4 at Philadelphia 5
April 30 Philadelphia 0 at Buffalo 3
        |Miller|
May 2 Buffalo 7 at Philadelphia 1
Buffalo wins best-of-seven 4–2

Western Conference Quarter-finals

April 21 Edmonton 2 at Detroit 3
        (Maltby 2:39 2OT)
April 23 Edmonton 4 at Detroit 2
April 25 Detroit 2 at Edmonton 3
        (Stoll 8:44 2OT)
April 27 Detroit 4 at Edmonton 2
April 29 Edmonton 3 at Detroit 2
May 1 Detroit 3 at Edmonton 4
Edmonton wins best-of-seven 4–2

April 22 Colorado 5 at Dallas 2
April 24 Colorado 5 at Dallas 4
        (Sakic 4:36 OT)
April 26 Dallas 3 at Colorado 4
        (Tanguay 1:09 OT)
April 28 Dallas 4 at Colorado 1
April 30 Colorado 3 at Dallas 2
        (Brunette 13:55 OT)
Colorado wins best-of-seven 4–1

April 21 Anaheim 1 at Calgary 2
        (McCarty 9:45 OT)
April 23 Anaheim 4 at Calgary 3
April 25 Calgary 5 at Anaheim 2
April 27 Calgary 2 at Anaheim 3
        (O'Donnell 1:36 OT)
April 29 Anaheim 2 at Calgary 3
May 1 Calgary 1 at Anaheim 2
May 3 Anaheim 3 at Calgary 0
        |Bryzgalov|
Anaheim wins best-of-seven 4–3

April 21 San Jose 3 at Nashville 4
April 23 San Jose 3 at Nashville 0
|Toskala|
April 25 Nashville 1 at San Jose 4
April 27 Nashville 4 at San Jose 5
April 30 San Jose 2 at Nashville 1
San Jose wins best-of-seven 4–1

Eastern Conference Semi-finals

May 5 Buffalo 7 at Ottawa 6
        (Drury 0:18 OT)
May 8 Buffalo 2 at Ottawa 1
May 10 Ottawa 2 at Buffalo 3
        (Dumont 5:05 OT)
May 11 Ottawa 2 at Buffalo 1
May 13 Buffalo 3 at Ottawa 2
        (Pominville 2:26 sh OT)
Buffalo wins best-of-seven 4–1

May 6 New Jersey 0 at Carolina 6
May 8 New Jersey 2 at Carolina 3
        (Wallin 3:09 OT)
May 10 Carolina 3 at New Jersey 2
May 13 Carolina 1 at New Jersey 5
May 14 New Jersey 1 at Carolina 4
Carolina wins best-of-seven 4–1

Western Conference Semi-finals

May 7 Edmonton 1 at San Jose 2
May 8 Edmonton 1 at San Jose 2
May 10 San Jose 2 at Edmonton 3
        (Horcoff 42:24 OT)
May 12 San Jose 3 at Edmonton 6
May 14 Edmonton 6 at San Jose 3
May 17 San Jose 0 at Edmonton 2
        |Roloson|
Edmonton wins best-of-seven 4–2

May 5 Colorado 0 at Anaheim 5
        |Bryzgalov|
May 7 Colorado 0 at Anaheim 3
        |Bryzgalov|
May 9 Anaheim 4 at Colorado 3
        (Lupul 16:30 OT)
May 11 Anaheim 4 at Colorado 1
Anaheim wins best-of-seven 4–0

Eastern Conference Finals

May 20 Buffalo 3 at Carolina 2
May 22 Buffalo 3 at Carolina 4
May 24 Carolina 3 at Buffalo 4
May 26 Carolina 4 at Buffalo 0
        |Gerber|
May 28 Buffalo 3 at Carolina 4
        (Stillman 8:46 pp OT)
May 30 Carolina 1 at Buffalo 2
        (Briere 4:22 pp OT)
June 1 Buffalo 2 at Carolina 4
Carolina wins best-of-seven 4–3

Western Conference Finals

May 19 Edmonton 3 at Anaheim 1
May 21 Edmonton 3 at Anaheim 1
May 23 Anaheim 4 at Edmonton 5
May 25 Anaheim 6 at Edmonton 3
May 27 Edmonton 2 at Anaheim 1
Edmonton wins best-of-seven 4–1

Stanley Cup Finals

June 5 Edmonton 4 at Carolina 5
June 7 Edmonton 0 at Carolina 5
June 10 Carolina 1 at Edmonton 2
June 12 Carolina 2 at Edmonton 1
June 14 Edmonton 4 at Carolina 3 (OT)
June 17 Carolina 0 at Edmonton 4
June 19 Edmonton 1 at Carolina 3
Carolina wins best-of-seven 4-3

2006 Edmonton Oilers Playoff Statistics

	GP	G	A	P	Pim
Chris Pronger	24	5	16	21	26
Shawn Horcoff	24	7	12	19	12
Fernando Pisani	24	14	4	18	10
Ales Hemsky	24	6	11	17	14
Ryan Smyth	24	7	9	16	22
Sergei Samsonov	24	4	11	15	14
Jaroslav Spacek	24	3	11	14	24
Michael Peca	24	6	5	11	20
Raffi Torres	22	4	7	11	16
Jarret Stoll	24	4	6	10	24
Steve Staios	24	1	5	6	28
Jason Smith	24	1	4	5	16
Rem Murray	24	0	4	4	2
Ethan Moreau	21	2	1	3	19
Marc-Andre Bergeron	18	2	1	3	14
Brad Winchester	10	1	2	3	4
Georges Laraque	15	1	1	2	44
Todd Harvey	10	1	1	2	4
Dwayne Roloson	18	0	2	2	14
Dick Tarnstrom	12	0	2	2	10
Radek Dvorak	16	0	2	2	4
Toby Petersen	2	1	0	1	0
Matt Greene	18	0	1	1	34
Jussi Markkanen	6	0	0	0	0
Ty Conklin	1	0	0	0	0

Goalies

	GP	W-L	Mins	GA	SO	GAA
Dwayne Roloson	18	12-5	1,159	45	1	2.33
Jussi Markkanen	6	3-3	360	13	0	2.17
Ty Conklin	1	0-1	5	1	0	12.00

right. On the plus side for Edmonton, the Oilers felt that they had speed and youth on their side while the Wings, experienced, yes, were a little long in the tooth, as it were.

The way game one played out, however, the odds got better for the Wings and worse for the Oilers. Kirk Maltby was credited with the winning goal at 2:39 of the second overtime period, but it was hardly a great goal. He had the puck along the boards and simply fired it toward the Edmonton goal. The puck hit Rem Murray's stick in front and deflected between the pads of a surprised Dwayne Roloson to give the Wings the opening game by a 3–2 score.

Detroit outshot Edmonton 57–25, and that was the stat that mattered more to the Oilers than the score. The Oilers played trap hockey in a strategic attempt to negate the superior team, and they got great defence and even greater goaltending. Roloson was heroic in goal, time and again coming up with a big save to keep his team in a game they had no right sending to overtime. In fact, it was the Wings that had to rally in the third to tie the score.

Robert Lang score the game's first goal, a Detroit score that came on a power play at 4:05 of the first period with Marc-Andre Bergeron in the penalty box. The Oilers responded with their own extra-man goal, Sergei Samsonov converting a pass from Ales Hemsky midway through the period. Despite being outshot 15–5, the Oilers headed to the dressing room tied 1–1.

In the second, another period dominated by the hometown Wings at the Joe Louis Arena, the Oilers took the lead on a power play. Chris Pronger's slapshot beat goalie Manny Legace, and the only goal of the middle period belonged to those 35–1 underdogs. It was up to Maltby to provide the heroics in regulation, as he shoved in a loose puck at 13:43 of the third to tie the game. The

Detroit's Daniel Cleary jumps for joy as Kirk Maltby's shot beats Dwayne Roloson in the second overtime to give Detroit a 1–0 series lead.

Oilers had a great chance to win the game when Brendan Shanahan was given a roughing penalty at 18:10, but they couldn't beat Legace as time wound down.

The first overtime was all Detroit, and Roloson kept the score 2–2 with some fine saves under tremendous pressure. He didn't fare so well on Draper's second goal of the game. Total shots in OT were 19–6 for Detroit, but the Oilers skated off after the loss knowing they could skate with the Wings and compete with a team that had played at a consistently higher level all season.

Game Two
April 23, 2006
Edmonton 4 at Detroit 2

Dwayne Roloson continued his great play despite a couple of whacky goals, and the hero of game one turned out to be the goat of game two. As a result, the Oilers headed back to Rexall Place tied 1–1 with the mighty Red Wings after a stunning and effective 4–2 victory. Fernando Pisani scored the game-tying goal late in the second period. Linemate Michael Peca stripped Kirk Maltby of the puck and passed to Pisani at the top of Manny Legace's crease,

and Pisani made no mistake with the in-close chance. It was Maltby who tied the game in the third period of game one and scored the winner in overtime.

The winning goal of game two came just 57 seconds later on another uncharacteristic turnover by the Wings. Chris Pronger took the puck off the stick of Jason Williams at the Detroit blueline and passed to Brad Winchester, and the youngster wired a shot past Legace to give Edmonton a 3–2 lead. It was his first career NHL goal. Winchester was a surprise starter. He played only 19 games all season and was dressing

for his first career playoff game this night. Coach Craig MacTavish played a hunch which turned out to be wisdom personified. Winchester played on a line with Shawn Horcoff and Ryan Smyth all night.

Both goals were the result of a more concerted effort to forecheck more aggressively, a way of augmenting the trap system the Oilers used to good effect in game one. The way the team played in this win, however, was important not just for the score but for the way it was accomplished. There was no lucky bounce or series of penalties to help their cause, only good, smart hockey

Fernando Pisani scores the tying goal in the second period en route to a 4–2 Oilers' victory in game two.

Henrik Zetterberg gets to the loose puck after goalie Dwayne Roloson lost sight of it and scores easily to make it 2–1 Detroit.

which led them to believe they could win every game like this.

Pronger got the Oilers on the board midway through the first period, but Williams tied the score on a flukey goal two minutes later. A pass out front hit Williams's skate just as Roloson left that side of the net, and the puck caromed in the small opening to the back side. The Wings took the lead in the second on an even luckier goal. Henrik Zetterberg's shot was stopped by Roloson, but he didn't see the puck bounce in the air, deflect off his helmet, and fall in behind him. Zetterberg was there to knock in the free puck to give Detroit a 2–1 lead on a pair of weird goals.

Undaunted, the Oilers stuck to their game plan and were rewarded with two late goals on turnovers. In the third, Roloson remained calm despite his team being outshot 14–8, and it was Edmonton that scored the only goal of the period, that an empty netter by Jarret Stoll in the final minute. Both Steve Yzerman and Henrik Zetterberg had breakaways in the third, but Yzerman hit the post and Roloson stoned Zetterberg.

Game Three
April 25, 2006
Detroit 3 at **Edmonton 4** (2OT)

With this overtime victory, the Oilers were now fully aware they could beat Detroit. Dwayne Roloson was again the hero at one end, stopping 44 of 47 Red Wings shots, and Jarret Stoll was the hero at the other end, scoring the winner 8:44 into the second extra period. He scooped a rebound after Manny Legace had made the original stop on a Sergei Samsonov shot and made no mistake.

For Edmonton, it was a game that confirmed its trap system was working on several fronts. One, it demanded an aggressive forecheck to pressure the puck carrier deep in his own end. Two, it negated Detroit's speed coming out of its own end. Three, it got the entire Oilers roster to buy into a team game. Lastly, the result tonight was typical of what the Oilers had done all year. They blew a third-period lead, but never gave up.

Jaroslav Spacek got the Oilers rolling with a goal early in the first period on a wrist shot, but this was negated midway through by Henrik Zetterberg. Edmonton took control of the game and the series with a pair of goals, one late in the first, the other early in the second. Ryan Smyth and Raffi Torres were the scorers, and with those goals the Oilers had a commanding two-goal lead for the first time in the playoffs.

The Oilers sat back, though, and the desperate Red Wings went all out in the third. The result was a pair of quick goals to shock the Oilers' fans. Zetterberg scored his second at 11:52 into a wide-open net after a great fake by Jason Williams who then passed across to Zetterberg. Just 18 seconds later, Mathieu Schneider tied the game on a slapshot off a faceoff, Yzerman winning the puck cleanly back to his defenceman.

Captain Steve Yzerman of Detroit sweeps around on his backhand for a shot, but goalie Dwayne Roloson is waiting for him and makes the save.

Tomas Holmstrom tries to screen Roloson who manages to make the save despite the distraction.

The Red Wings thought they had won the game late in the first overtime. Williams's shot seemed to go in, but video review showed the puck slid under the side of the net when Roloson backed up and lifted the goal ever so slightly.

In the first overtime, the Oilers had one power play and Detroit two, but neither team could convert on a game-winning man advantage. In all, both teams had nine power plays, Edmonton scoring twice and the Red Wings once. By the end of the game, the news for Detroit was doubly bad: the Wings lost the contest, but their longtime captain Steve Yzerman left the game in the first OT with a bad back and was a questionable starter for game four. Defenceman Chris Pronger was utterly remarkable for the Oilers, playing more than 47 minutes and finishing +1.

Game Four

April 27, 2006

Detroit 4 at Edmonton 2

In what was almost a do-or-die game for Detroit, the visiting Wings rallied for a critical 4–2 win to even their best-of-seven series, 2–2. Had they lost and trailed the series 3–1, elimination would almost surely have been inevitable. Impressively, they won without captain Steve Yzerman who decided just before the game that his back was too sore to play.

As in the previous game, this was marred by a seemingly endless stream of minor penalties for obstruction of one sort or another. By the end of the night, the stats read eleven power plays for Detroit, converting on three, while Edmonton

Edmonton's Fernando Pisani high sticks Mikael Samuelsson in the third period and incurs a penalty for his actions.

Robert Lang of Detroit and Raffi Torres get mixed up along the boards during third-period action.

had two goals on eight chances.

The Oilers got the game's first goal thanks to some fine work by Raffi Torres. He carried the puck in over the Detroit blueline, taking two defenders with him, before passing off to Fernando Pisani. Pisani ripped a shot from the right faceoff circle that beat Manny Legace cleanly. The Wings dominated the period, though, and scored twice before the first intermission. Tomas Holmstrom tied the game at 13:25 on a 5-on-3. He stood at the top of Dwayne Roloson's crease and tipped a Mathieu Schneider shot past the screened goalie. Robert Lang scored

a huge goal for Detroit at 19:23 when his shot banked off the skate of Jaroslav Spacek and in. The goal sent his team to the dressing room ahead by a 2–1 count.

Edmonton scored the only goal of the second period with Kirk Maltby in the penalty box. Jaroslav Spacek took a cross-ice feed from Ales Hemsky and blew a one-timer past Legace to send the crowd into a frenzy.

Detroit scored the go-ahead goal in the third, though, on another 5-on-3. This time it was Nicklas Lidstrom's shot that beat Roloson. A few minutes later, Ryan Smyth thought he scored the tying goal.

He tried a wraparound on Legace, but the goalie got his glove on the puck before it crossed the goal line. Video replay confirmed the save, and the Oilers lost their chance. Henrik Zetterberg completed the scoring with a late backhand goal, also on the power play.

The series was going back to Detroit tied 2–2, the Wings having re-gained home-ice advantage but the Oilers confident they could win if they stuck to their game plan. It worked very well in games two and three, but in game four Detroit used its speed to draw penalties and kill the Oilers on the power play.

Game Five
April 29, 2006
Edmonton 3 at Detroit 2

The Dwayne Roloson Show reached its climax in the first period of this series-turning game. While the Oilers took four penalties in the opening 20 minutes, playing short-handed for eight of those minutes, Roloson was perfect, stopping all eleven shots he faced and keeping the game scoreless after one period when the Wings clearly deserved to be in the lead. The rest of his Edmonton team took that performance to heart and scored three times in the second on the way to victory in Detroit. The goals came in a seven-minute stretch that left the Red Wings reeling.

Fernando Pisani, Ryan Smyth, and Shawn Horcoff scored the goals, the last of which was a lucky one. Horcoff's initial shot was stopped by Manny Legace, but Detroit defenceman Niklas Kronwall smacked the puck into his own goal

Ryan Smyth (#94) and Michael Peca congratulate goalie Dwayne Roloson after the team's victory in game five.

Detroit defender Niklas Kronwall has Shawn Horcoff's shot bounce off his skate and past Manny Legace in the second period.

in an effort to clear the rebound. Pisani made a nice deflection off a Chris Pronger point shot, and Jarret Stoll's shot hit Smyth and went in.

Brendan Shanahan tried to breathe some life into the Detroit offence with a late goal in the second on a hard wrist shot, but the Oilers refused to give in. Detroit controlled the third period, but mostly from the outside. Henrik Zetterberg made the score close when his slapshot beat Roloson with 22 seconds left in the game, but the Oilers hung on for the win and headed home with a 3–2 lead in the series and a chance to eliminate the NHL's top regular-season team two nights later.

CONFERENCE SEMI-FINALS—Edmonton vs. Detroit Red Wings

69

Game Six
May 1, 2006
Detroit 3 at Edmonton 4

Despite outshooting Edmonton for the sixth straight game, Detroit found itself shaking hands with the Oilers after being eliminated by the heavy underdogs. Although the hero of the series was clearly goalie Dwayne Roloson, the hero of the night was Ales Hemsky who broke a 3–3 tie with a goal just 1:06 from the end of the third period after a give-and-go with Sergei Samsonov.

Less than two minutes earlier, Hemsky had scored the tying goal as well on an odd play. A power-play shot hit Shawn Horcoff and the puck landed at Hemsky's feet. As he tried to take a quick shot, Detroit defenceman Nicklas Lidstrom checked him, but he drove Hemsky into the net and with him the puck. Video review concluded Hemsky didn't kick the puck in, and the goal stood. The game also featured a remarkable rally by Edmonton, trailing 2–0 after two periods—or, from the opposite perspective, a remarkable collapse by the Wings. The Oilers were on to the second round of the playoffs for the first time since 1998.

The game began mirror opposite to the previous five. This time, it was the Oilers that came out flying and applied pressure on Detroit for the first 20 minutes, but it was Red Wings goalie Manny Legace who stole the show, stopping all 15 Edmonton shots and giving his team some much needed confidence. Henrik Zetterberg scored the only goal of the opening period and Robert Lang scored the only goal of the second on a power play.

Yet in the dressing room before the third period, it was the Oilers that felt relaxed and confident and the more experienced Wings tense. The Oilers came out flying once

Steve Yzerman and Ales Hemsky battle for a loose puck early in the decisive game. Was this Stevie Y's final NHL game?

Detroit goalie Manny Legace gives his Edmonton counterpart Dwayne Roloson a hug and congratulations on a series well won.

again and tied the game inside seven minutes. Fernando Pisani scored both goals, the first on a nice deke of Legace, the second after controlling a rebound in tight.

Johan Franzen restored the lead for Detroit at 10:07 on a rebound, but then Hemsky went to work. Held goalless in the first five games, he scored twice in the final four minutes. The game winner came after a great pass through the crease by Sergei Samsonov, and Hemsky, parked at Legace's back door, knocked the puck over the goal line to send the Rexall Place fans into celebration mode.

Try as they might in the final minute, the Wings couldn't tie the game, and captain Steve Yzerman, who was playing with an extremely sore back, headed off the ice for what might have been the last time of his extraordinary career. The Oilers, meanwhile, slept in their own beds and prepared to face the San Jose Sharks in the Conference semi-finals.

Conference Semi-finals
Edmonton Oilers vs. San Jose Sharks

Game One
May 7, 2006
Edmonton 1 at San Jose 2

The Oilers may have eliminated the league's top team, but they were still very much underdogs when they traveled to San Jose to face the Sharks. The Sharks, after all, had the league's top point getter (Joe Thornton, 125) and top goal scorer (Jonathan Cheechoo, 56), two breakout players who could take

a close game and blow it open with one awesome shift.

San Jose came out in game one and made a point right away when Cheechoo nailed the Oilers' star defenceman Chris Pronger with a hard, clean check that sent Pronger to the ice on his first shift. That's the way it was all night. Ville Nieminen led all players in hits, and his abrasive style followed Cheechoo's hit and set the tone. The Sharks played a bigger, faster, more physical

game than the Oilers, who realized once again they'd have to raise their game another level if they were going to avoid being embarrassed by the Sharks. By the end of the night, it was clear San Jose was a more formidable opponent, and the 2–1 score flattered the Oilers.

Despite having a horrible 1–18 success rate against San Jose on the power play during the regular season, the Oilers score the opening goal early in the first with the extra

Radek Dvorak makes a spectacular attempt to score on a wraparound on San Jose goalie Vesa Toskala.

Joe Thornton, Art Ross Trophy winner, is stopped cold by Roloson in the first period.

man. Jaroslav Spacek one-timed a perfect cross-ice pass from Ales Hemsky, and his shot beat Vesa Toskala at 2:33. The Sharks came back a few minutes later, tying the game on a similar play. Steve Bernier threaded a pass to Patrick Marleau, and his quick shot in the slot got by Dwayne Roloson before the goalie could grab it.

The second and third periods belonged to the Sharks. They allowed just seven shots over the final 40 minutes, and although they scored just once, they had several fine chances and outshot Edmonton 30–16. Christian Ehrhoff scored the eventual winning goal early in the second when his slapshot from the point beat Roloson high. With that goal, the Sharks gained confidence

and went to the attack with renewed energy. Instead of sitting on the lead, they pressed and skated hard on offence, and only Roloson and a bit of bad luck prevented them from scoring three or four more goals. The Sharks won for the 12th time in their past 14 games, including an elimination of first-round opponents Nashville in just five games.

Game Two

May 8, 2006

Edmonton 1 at San Jose 2

It was the same score as game one, and it was more of the same from the Sharks in every aspect of play. They were the better team, skated harder, hit harder, and played smarter defence. In the end, it was another one-goal game that wasn't as close as the scoreboard suggested.

This time it was the Sharks that got the early goal. Tom Priessing scored at 4:26 on a scramble in the crease to spot the Sharks a quick 1–0 lead at HP Pavilion, a goal that stood up until late in the second period. In between, the Oilers had to kill of a series of penalties. Midway through the first, both Raffi Torres and Jarret Stoll were in the box, but their teammates killed off that 5-on-3 successfully. Later, the Oilers were down a man again, but

Raffi Torres of Edmonton tackles Nils Ekman in front of Oilers' goalie Dwayne Roloson.

San Jose's Grant Stevenson falls awkwardly into the gate after being checked by Brad Winchester.

they escaped the first period trailing by just the one goal.

Sergei Samsonov gave the Oilers hope when he scored late in the second by scooping a rebound no one else saw, but any momentum the Oilers hoped to gain from this goal was nullified by two penalties. The Sharks cashed in on the first of those when Joe Thornton, goalless through the first six games of the playoffs, beat Dwayne Roloson with a shot along the ice from near the end red line. It was a great goal that started when a rebound came right to him, chest high. He gloved the puck, placed it on the ice, and shot in one swift motion. Three seconds after the faceoff, the Oilers were penalized again, but they survived this scare and headed to the dressing room down only 2–1.

As in game one, the Sharks drew confidence from the go-ahead goal and they again dominated the third period, not allowing the Oilers any breathing room or chance to tie the game. Roloson was great again in goal, facing 38 Sharks shots, and San Jose limited their opponents to just two power-play chances. That was the kind of discipline that won hockey games—and the Oilers were finding that out the hard way.

Game Three
May 10, 2006
San Jose 2 at **Edmonton 3** (3OT)

It was a make or break game for the Oilers. A loss would have dropped them down three games to the Sharks, a situation that would have virtually guaranteed elimination. Instead, however, they came away with a victory, a heart-stopping victory that took nearly two full games of hockey. Shawn Horcoff scored the winning goal 2:24 into the third overtime period after taking a beautiful touch backhand pass from Ryan Smyth behind the Sharks' net. It was Edmonton's 58th shot of the game on Vesa Toskala, but it gave the Oilers the win and that was all that mattered.

Unlike the previous two games, the Oilers played with greater poise and discipline. In the first period, they drew the only two penalties and scored the only goal with one of those man advantages. Marc-Andre Bergeron scored first on a shot from the slot with Alyn McCauley in the penalty box, but it was the second period that defined the game in many ways.

For starters, the Sharks scored twice to take the lead. Patrick Marleau scored just 1:19 into the period when Roloson couldn't control Josh

Marc-Andre Bergeron delivers a textbook example of a hip check in sending the Sharks' Grant Stevenson through the air.

Pat Rismiller beats Dwayne Roloson to give his Sharks an early 2–0 lead in game three.

Gorges' point shot, and then Pat Rismiller scored midway through after taking a pinpoint pass from Joe Thornton. Both teams, however, took potentially harmful penalties. For the Sharks, they received three goaltender interference penalties in a span of eight minutes. After the game, Sharks coach Ron Wilson accused Oilers' goalie Dwayne Roloson of grandstanding, of embellishing every incidental contact, of goading the referees into calling the penalties.

For the Oilers, they ran into serious trouble at 13:38 when Georges Laraque was assessed a boarding major and game misconduct for his vicious hit from behind on Jonathan Cheechoo. The Oilers withstood the extended power play, cut short by one of the three goalie interference penalties, but it could have been a series-ending major penalty had the Sharks been able to capitalize.

As it was, Edmonton entered the third period down a goal, and at 13:13 the home side tied the game on a Raffi Torres shot. The play started behind the Edmonton goal where Chris Pronger made a long pass to Jarret Stoll, and Stoll hit Torres as he accelerated through centre ice and moved in on goal. He let go a perfect snapshot that beat Toskala cleanly.

The first overtime was played mostly in the San Jose end, and the Oilers had a power play when Christian Ehrhoff took a holding penalty, but teams headed to their rooms after 80 minutes still tied. In the fifth period, the referees gave the Sharks a man advantage late, but they, too, failed to score. That penalty to Jarret Stoll carried over into the sixth period, and soon after Stoll came out of the box, Horcoff scored the winning goal. The Oilers left the ice exhausted but victorious; the Sharks left still in the series lead but with their confidence shaken.

Game Four
May 12, 2006
San Jose 3 at **Edmonton 6**

A good bounce, a few breaks, a never-say-die attitude, and by the end of it all the Oilers had a convincing 6–3 win under their belt and psychologically were the stronger team. It was a game that started out like another San Jose victory, but for the first time in the playoffs the team received some spotty goaltending from Vesa Toskala and the Oilers rallied from 2–0 and 3–1 deficits to win.

The game was less than seven minutes old by the time the Sharks were up a pair of goals, scoring on their only two shots to that point in the game. Joe Thornton and Nils Ekman were the scorers. On the first goal, it was Ekman who outwaited Edmonton defenceman Jarosav Spacek on a two-on-one before sliding a pass to Thornton at the side of the goal. Ekman made it 2–0 himself when he one-timed a Patrick Marleau pass to perfection, and the packed house in Edmonton watched in silence as the Sharks played with a control that defined their first two wins.

Shawn Horcoff got the Oilers—and their fans—back into the game with a goal six minutes after Ekman's, but Jonathan Cheechoo scored his third of the playoffs midway through the second to restore the two-goal San Jose advantage. Then things went Edmonton's way. Michael Peca scored a weak goal on Toskala, finding the net from a bad angle on a shot the goalie should have handled.

A minute later, though, Sergei Samsonov was penalized at 13:29. At the end of a successful kill of that penalty the Oilers dumped the puck out of their end just as Samsonov returned to the ice. The puck rolled toward Toskala who came well out to try to beat Samsonov to the puck, but he cleared it right into the body

Joe Thornton opens the scoring early in the first period, beating Dwayne Roloson, but the Oilers prevailed, 6–3.

The Oilers celebrate their fourth goal early in the third period which turned out to be the game winner.

of the oncoming forward. The puck squirted free, and Samsonov had an empty net for the tying goal.

The third period was controlled by Edmonton. The Oilers scored the only three goals of the final 20 minutes, the first of those—the game winner—coming from captain and defenceman Jason Smith who recorded his first career playoff goal. He took a pass from Samsonov in the Sharks end, and like Bobby Orr

went to the net with the puck where he calmly lifted a backhand past Toskala.

Ales Hemsky made it 5–3 a few minutes later when he skated hard to the net while Ryan Smyth carried the puck down the left wing. Smyth waited, and as Hemsky arrived at the crease he threw a hard pass at the net that Hemsky merely tipped past the goalie. That goal spelled the end for Toskala who was relieved by

Evgeni Nabokov. Jarret Stoll added a power-play goal at 14:00 to round out the scoring.

When all was said and done, it was a convincing victory to tie the series 2–2, in part because of the comeback, in part because the Oilers finally shook the confidence of the previously unflappable Toskala, in part because they went to the net with confidence and created their own good fortune.

Game Five

May 14, 2006

Edmonton 6 at San Jose 3

The first half of the script was like the one from the previous game, but in reverse; the second half was identical. This time, the Oilers blew a 3–1 lead, but once again they reeled off three, third-period goals to pull away with the win and take control of the series, now leading 3–2.

It was a game that was marred by the booing of O *Canada* by the sold-out HP Pavilion crowd despite the fact that half of their own San Jose team was comprised of Canadian players, but by the end of the game it was the home side, not the Canadian team, that had earned the boos. The next day, San Jose mayor Ron Gonzales apologized for the boorish behaviour of the local fans.

Unlike so many games this year for Edmonton, the Oilers cashed in on their power plays and the Sharks were undone by the Oilers' penalty killing. Edmonton scored on three of seven chances, while the Sharks were shut out on their seven chances. In the five games, in fact, the Oilers killed off 25 of 27 short-handed situations against San Jose.

Fernando Pisani got the only goal of the first period with the teams playing 5-on-5. The Oilers killed off three minors in that 20 minutes and were outshot 9–4, but they led 1–0 until early in the second when Scott Thornton tied the game off a passing play with Christian Ehrhoff and Sascha Goc. Ryan Smyth restored the Edmonton lead at 6:31 on the

Edmonton's behemoth defenceman Chris Pronger crashes into the boards with the Sharks' Nils Ekman.

Fernando Pisani's shot beat Vesa Toskala, the only goal of the first period.

power play, and the Oilers killed off four more penalties to frustrate one of the most potent offences in the league during the regular season.

Shawn Horcoff scored what should have been the key goal, beating Vesa Toskala just 12 seconds into the third period while the Oilers were playing short-handed. Instead, the goal had the opposite effect, starting a flurry of activity that saw the Sharks tie the game before the Oilers took control. Ehrhoff and Jonathan Cheechoo scored within two minutes to make the score 3–3, but Fernando Pisani came right back to score the go-ahead goal at 4:03.

Then the Sharks collapsed. They spent most of the last half of the period killing off five penalties, and the Oilers took advantage to score twice with the extra man to close out the game with a 6–3 victory. Jarret Stoll and Ryan Smyth scored the late goals. The Oilers beat Toskala six times on just 18 shots, and it was the Sharks, once leading the series 2–0, that had lost three straight and were now on the verge of elimination.

CONFERENCE SEMI-FINALS—Edmonton vs. San Jose Sharks

81

Game Six
May 17, 2006

San Jose 0 at **Edmonton 2**

The series came full circle in game six as it was now the Oilers that played superb defence, limited the scoring chances of the Sharks, and capitalized on their chances to win, 2–0. They eliminated San Jose and advanced to the Conference finals for the first time since 1992, and were now set to face Anaheim which had disposed of Colorado in four straight games.

As had been the case all playoffs, goalie Dwayne Roloson was the main star for Edmonton, blocking 24 shots and earning his first career playoff shutout. Michael Peca scored in the first period and Shawn Horcoff in the third for the Oilers who did a great job of shutting down San Jose's big three weapons—Joe Thornton, Jonathan Cheechoo, and Patrick Marleau. Tonight, the second story was the Edmonton penalty killers who handled all eight man disadvantages successfully and gave up just two goals in 35 chances in the series.

Peca's goal came after some diligent checking. He stripped Scott Hannan of the puck near centre ice and waltzed in alone on Vesa Toskala, making no mistake with

Mark Smith of the Sharks crashes into Edmonton goalie Dwayne Roloson in the first period.

Michael Peca celebrates his first-period goal with the help of fans at Rexall Place.

his shot. In the third, it was puck pressure in the San Jose end that led to Horcoff's goal at 11:37. Todd Harvey got possession of the puck in the corner and spotted Horcoff alone in front of Toskala. He calmly roofed a shot over the sprawling goalie. That goal gave the Oilers a bit of a cushion, but they made life difficult for themselves trying to hold that lead, twice having to kill penalties in the final minutes to preserve the win and shutout.

The Sharks started the series with such impressive dominance, but the Oilers quickly reversed the course of action and it was Edmonton that finished with equal dominance and advanced to the next round. For the Sharks, they could only wonder at what they did so well in the first two games but couldn't replicate the rest of the series.

Conference Finals
Edmonton Oilers vs. Mighty Ducks of Anaheim

Game One
May 19, 2006
Edmonton 3 at Anaheim 1

The Oilers were playing the first game of this series after just two days' rest; the Mighty Ducks had a ten-day layoff. The result was a routine and unspectacular 3–1 win by the more charged Edmontons over the rusty Ducks. In this sense, though, the result gave the Oilers confidence that they now had a system down so pat that it could take them as far as they believed—and they believed plenty.

Dwayne Roloson not only continued his fine play in goal for the Oilers, he also produced a great long-bomb pass to set up the game's first goal. With Chris Pronger serving a two-minute penalty for elbowing, Roloson caught sight of Michael Peca breaking out his end while the goalie had the puck. Roloson fired a long, high pass that Peca controlled, and he went in on goal to beat Ilya Bryzgalov with a deke before tucking the puck between the goalie's pads. Seconds later, though, the Ducks tied the game on that same power

Michael Peca beats Anaheim goalie Ilya Bryzgalov on a short-handed breakaway to give the Oilers an early 1–0 lead.

Goalie Dwayne Roloson loses his mask but keeps his eye on the puck after making a save.

play, Andy McDonald's high shot catching Roloson off guard.

Ales Hemsky put the Oilers up for good midway through the second period on a power play. Ryan Smyth took the initial shot, and Bryzgalov made the save, but the goalie couldn't control the rebound. Hemsky batted the puck in before anyone could check him. The Oilers added an empty netter in the final minute of the third with Bryzgalov on the bench for a sixth attacker after the Ducks had peppered Roloson with 14 shots in an effort to tie the game.

The Oilers' special teams were fast becoming their most important strength after the play of Roloson. They limited Anaheim to one goal on eight power-play chances, and, of course, scored the short-handed goal to get things going. It wasn't the most impressive win in the playoffs, but they all count and the Oilers returned to their hotel rooms in Newport Beach, California, with a one-game lead in the series for the first time this spring.

Game Two
May 21, 2006
Edmonton 3 at Anaheim 1

All the signs were good ones for Edmonton after taking a 2–0 lead in the series with a pair of road victories. Historically, the franchise was 18–0 in playoff series they led 2–0. The last time they were up 2–0 on the road, they won the Stanley Cup. They were unbeaten against Anaheim in six games this season. And, Anaheim had never rallied from 2–0 down to win a series in its brief NHL history.

Despite outshooting the Oilers 34–25 in game two, the Ducks were outdone by Edmonton goalie Dwayne Roloson and the Oilers' penalty killing. Worse, the Oilers were playing with more and more confidence after their sixth straight win in these playoffs. And this despite a team weakened by a flu bug that was making its way through the dressing room and sickening many players.

Chris Pronger put the Oilers on the scoresheet first with a power-play goal at 13:08 of the first period thanks to another of his booming slapshots, and they took that one-goal lead to the dressing room. In the second, Jeff Friesen tied the game early on when he converted a Rob Niedermayer pass after an Edmonton giveaway, a rare error by the Oilers. Friesen made a nice deke in tight and slid the puck in the open side after drawing Roloson out of position.

Fernando Pisani put the Oilers in the lead again at 17:09 on another turnover, this by Anaheim's Teemu Selanne who was stripped of the puck by Sergei Samsonov. Pisani ripped a shot past Ilya Bryzgalov that hit the crossbar and deflected down into the goal. Anaheim did everything it could to tie the game in the final period, but Roloson was unbeatable. Michael Peca added a goal into the empty net with Bryzgalov on the bench for the Ducks. Roloson was credited with an assist on the Peca goal, giving him two helpers in as many games.

Ales Hemsky can't corral the puck long enough to beat Ilya Bryzgalov on this first-period power play for the Oilers.

Oilers' forward Georges Laraque avoids a hit from Vitali Vishnevski of the Ducks.

CONFERENCE FINALS—Edmonton vs. Mighty Ducks of Anaheim

87

Game Three
May 23, 2006
Anaheim 4 at **Edmonton 5**

Yes, the Oilers won the game to take a stranglehold in the series 3–0, but Anaheim showed enough character and life that if the Oilers felt the third game ensured them the series victory, they knew how wrong they could be. The Oilers were coasting along in the third period with an easy 4–0 lead, but by the final horn they were lucky to escape with the win. That's playoff hockey.

The significance of the game translated early on with tempers flaring on both benches. Todd Fedoruk and Georges Laraque each received five-minute fighting penalties at 2:51, and just 19 seconds later a scrum involving everyone on ice resulted in more penalties. Two minutes after that, another fight erupted between Anaheim's Joe DiPenta and Edmonton's Ethan Moreau, and with those pent-up hostilities out of the way the teams settled down to play emotional, hard-fought hockey.

Toby Petersen, the minor-leaguer, was in the lineup for Edmonton and scored the first and only goal of the opening period, and the second period failed to produce another goal either. There were plenty of minor penalties to go around, but both teams' power plays were held at bay by superior penalty killing and good goaltending from Dwayne Roloson in the Oilers' net and Ilya Bryzgalov at the other end.

All hell broke loose in the third. Michael Peca tipped the puck past a stationery Anaheim defenceman, Ruslan Salei, at the Oilers' blueline, and cruised in alone on Bryzgalov. Peca ripped a shot over the goalie's glove for his fourth goal in as many games. The Oilers made it 3–0 thanks to a highlight pass from Sergei Samsonov who held onto the puck as he cut through the slot and made a sensational back pass to Steve Staios who hammered it into the empty net. Chris Pronger made it 4–0 on a power

Anaheim goalie Ilya Bryzgalov makes a save while his defenceman Todd Fedoruk takes care of Georges Laraque in front.

Steve Staios (left) celebrates his goal to make it 3–0 with Jarret Stoll (right) and Sergei Samsonov.

play, another slapshot sizzler beating Bryzgalov cleanly.

Leading 4–0 with just over 15 minutes to go in the game, the Oilers figured they had the game won. They stopped skating, and worse, they stopped competing. The result was a near-miracle comeback by Anaheim. The Ducks got on the board at 7:15 thanks to Sean O'Donnell, made it 4–2 two minutes later on a Teemu Selanne goal, and drew within one at 11:15 after Chris Kunitz beat Roloson. O'Donnell's goal was a point shot that eluded Roloson, and Selanne scored after faking a shot and moving around the sliding defenceman Jaroslav Spacek before beating the goalie with a low shot.

The Oilers woke up just in time. Fernando Pisani put the Oilers up 5–3 after fighting off a check and making a great move on Bryzgalov, but even that was barely enough. Selanne scored again at 18:15, and a furious Anaheim assault almost produced the tying goal. The Ducks outshot Edmonton 16–8 in the third period and 38–22 overall but came away empty-handed again. They were 0–7 on the power play while Edmonton was 2–8.

CONFERENCE FINALS—Edmonton vs. Mighty Ducks of Anaheim

89

Game Four
May 25, 2006
Anaheim 6 at Edmonton 3

What a difference a couple of days make. This Anaheim team was as night-and-day better than it was in losing game three, and the Oilers were every bit as bad this night as they had been good in winning the first three games of the series. The result was a need for game five, which no longer seemed like a sure thing for the Oilers.

The Ducks began the first period like their season depended on it—and it did—outshooting Edmonton by a whopping count of 25–3 and outscoring them 3–0 to leave the Edmonton fans in stunned silence as they went for tissues, not champagne, at the first intermission. Goalie Dwayne Roloson, one of many Oilers suffering from the flu, headed for the washroom after 20 minutes, but after emptying the contents of his stomach into the toilet, he battled hard the rest of the way to show the kind of team spirit Edmonton needed in goal. Jean-Sebastien Giguere was getting his first start in the series, but it can't be said the goalie change made a difference. He had no difficult stops to make in the opening period.

Dustin Penner scored the first two goals for Anaheim and then Ryan Getzlaf added another at 19:18 on a one-timer on a power play in a period in which Edmonton served all five penalties assessed by the refereeing tandem of Paul Devosrki and Dan O'Halloran. Penner's first was the result of a rush by Teemu Selanne. His shot caromed off the skate of defenceman Jaroslav Spacek and into the net, but Penner was given credit.

Dwayne Roloson fails to stop this shot by Dustin Penner (out of frame) in the wild first period of game four.

Edmonton forward Ryan Smyth charges the net as goalie Jean-Sebastien Giguere stands his ground.

His second goal was of finer quality as he drilled a shot through traffic that missed Roloson and found the back of the net. Edmonton woke up in the second period and almost made a great comeback of it, but just as the Ducks fell short in game three, so, too, did the Oilers stall just shy of tying the game.

Marc-Andre Bergeron got an early goal in the second at 3:30 on Edmonton's first power play of the night, but Ruslan Salei made it 4–1 when his long wrist shot from the point made it through a maze of players and past Roloson. Ryan Smyth then made it 4–2 at 7:46 and less than three minutes later Georges Laraque scored his first goal of these playoffs to make it 4–3. He managed to control a rebound off a Chris Pronger point shot and made a nice move to put the puck into the open side of the net. The crowd was back in the game and the Oilers appeared to have recovered their senses, but the Ducks were not wavering.

Todd Marchant won a faceoff deep in the Edmonton end, and Joffrey Lupul's quick shot beat Roloson to make it a two-goal game again, 5–3. The Oilers had no energy to continue their attack in the third, and Lupul added his second of the night, this into an empty net, to finish the scoring and send the series back to California.

Game Five

May 27, 2006

Edmonton 2 at Anaheim 1

Building on their great victory two nights earlier, Anaheim came out storming in the first period again but couldn't maintain the momentum for long enough or build enough of a lead to win a second game. For the first time in the series, the team that didn't score first won the game, and with the victory the Oilers earned at least a week off to prepare for their first Stanley Cup finals since 1990 when they won the Cup.

The Oilers dodged a bullet on several fronts this night. Dwayne

Roloson stopped 32 of 33 shots as his team was outshot again, and the Oilers were short-handed eleven times to just six times for the Ducks. Edmonton failed to score on its man advantages, but more important the Oilers limited the Ducks to one power-play goal, that early in the first period by Francois Beauchemin. His slapshot from the point hit a body in front and fooled Roloson, but that was to be the last time the Oilers' goalie would be fooled in this series.

Edmonton got all the goals it needed in the second period. Ethan Moreau tied the score at 3:42. He tried to beat Jean-Sebastein Giguere on a wraparound, but the goalie covered the glove side to make the save. Giguere failed to control the puck, however, and it came right back to Moreau who calmly lifted it over the prone goalie.

Raffi Torres, who was so sick before game four that he was barred from the dressing room for fear of spreading his flu, was back in the lineup and scored the series winner a few minutes after Moreau's goal. He skated through the slot when Marc-Andre Bergeron let go a point shot, and he got enough of his stick on the puck to change its direction substantially. It went past Giguere, and the Oilers had a 2–1 lead.

There was still half a game left to be played, though, and it can't be said that the Oilers were impressive the rest of the way. They had to kill off six minor penalties in the second half of the game, the most important of which came late in the third.

Edmonton received a bench minor for too many men at 16:10, and then, while playing down a man, defenceman Chris Pronger cleared the puck over the glass to incur a delay of game penalty, leaving the Oilers two men short for 28 seconds and one man down for most of the rest of the game. The defence held,

Edmonton captain Jason Smith accepts the Clarence S. Campbell trophy without actually picking it up, a superstitious reminder that it's the Stanley Cup that his teammates want to hoist—and nothing else.

though, and even with Giguere on the bench for most of the last three minutes the Oilers refused to allow the tying goal. They won the game and series, and most important they won a few days off to recover from the flu bug before starting the Stanley Cup finals.

Stanley Cup Finals
Edmonton Oilers vs. Carolina Hurricanes

Game One
June 5, 2006
Edmonton 4 at Carolina 5

The number of story lines heading into this most unlikely of finals could have kept reporters busy for months. Unfortunately, they had but seven games at most to capture the essence of one of the oddest finals matchups of recent years.

There was the story of Edmonton defenceman Chris Pronger, who started his career with Hartford, the predecessor to Carolina. Carolina coach Peter Laviolette had one of his finest career moments with Oilers' backup goalie Ty Conklin at the 2004 World Championship where USA stunned the world with a bronze medal, a team coached by the 'Canes leader and featuring Conklin in goal. Carolina forward Ray Whitney was an Edmonton boy whose father, Floyd, has been a longtime practice goalie for the Oilers. Such was the nature of this series, though, that the Oilers actually barred Floyd from contact with the Oilers, for fear the old man might impart some words of wisdom to his son and the opposing team. Glen Wesley, at the start of his career, had played in two previous Cup finals against Edmonton while he was with Boston, losing in 1988 and again in 1990. Now nearing the end of his career, Wesley still had not won a Cup, and his 1,473 career games put him eighth all-time on a list of most games played without a championship.

With all this in mind, game one started in Carolina and proved to be a classic. Right from the opening faceoff both teams skated end-to-end, hitting each other hard but clean, and creating plenty of scoring chances. The Oilers showed no signs of rust from their lengthy layoff, and, in fact, looked more rested and polished than the Hurricanes. Fernando Pisani scored the only goal of the first period when he claimed a rebound left by Carolina goalie Cam Ward, and in the second period the visitors poured it on.

The Oilers made it 2–0 when defenceman Chris Pronger scored on a penalty shot. The play started when Carolina defenceman Niklas Wallin cleared the puck out of the

Fernando Pisani controls the rebound and puts the puck past Cam Ward for an early 1–0 Edmonton lead in game one.

crease with his glove, forcing referee Mick McGeough to call for a penalty shot. Coach Craig MacTavish could have chosen any player on ice to take the freebie, but with his fourth line out there he opted for his defenceman, a most unlikely choice. Pronger ripped a low wrist shot stick side with the poise and confidence of a sniper, and he became the first player in Cup finals history to score on a penalty shot.

Six minutes later, Edmonton made it 3–0 with shocking simplicity when an Ethan Moreau shot deflected in front and beat Ward. If the Oilers thought the lead was too easy to be true, they were right.

The turning point came late in the second when Edmonton goalie Dwayne Roloson was unable to handle a routine shot by Justin Williams. Rod Brind'Amour was standing beside the goalie and swiped the rebound into the open net, and with that Carolina was back in the game despite playing 40 dreadful minutes.

In the third, they came out like champions. Ray Whitney scored on a long-distance one-timer that Roloson might have had on another night, and Whitney tied the game three and a half minutes later on the power play with his second of the period. Five minutes later, the game unraveling at lightning speed for Edmonton, Steve Staios bobbled the puck at the Carolina blueline on a power play and Williams picked up the loose puck and skated in alone on Roloson. Like Pronger, he made no mistake with a low wrister stick side, and now, amazingly, the Hurricanes had a 4–3 lead.

The Oilers tied the game on a great pass from Jarret Stoll to Ales Hemsky as they entered the Carolina zone. Hemsky drove down the right wing, cut sharply across the crease, and slid the puck to the far side to tie the game 4–4 at 13:31.

The night's drama was only just beginning, though. While overtime

seemed likely, one play changed the course of the game and perhaps the series. Carolina's Andrew Ladd was driving hard to the net without the puck when he was checked by Edmonton defenceman Marc-Andre Bergeron who made the oft-repeated and horrible mistake of pushing the attacking player toward his own goalie. Ladd crashed into Roloson who was pushed back against the post. The goalie suffered a serious knee injury and an elbow injury to boot, and not only did he have to leave the game but he was deemed finished for the rest of the playoffs.

Conklin came in to finish the game, a game that ended in regulation thanks to an awful gaffe on the goalie's part. Playing a routine shoot-in behind his own goal, he fumbled the short pass to his defenceman Jason Smith and Rod Brind'Amour swept in between the two, took the puck and rammed it into the open

Chris Pronger celebrates his second-period goal on a penalty shot, the first in NHL Cup finals history.

net at 19:28. It was an absolutely stunning loss for a team that had played with such composure during the playoffs, but be that as it may, the Oilers had less than 48 hours to regain that composure and find a new number-one goalie.

Carolina's Andrew Ladd crashed into goalie Dwayne Roloson after being shoved by Marc-Andre Bergeron. Roloson suffered a series-ending knee injury on the play.

Game Two
June 7, 2006
Edmonton 0 at Carolina 5

In the hours and days leading up to game two, there was little talk about the drama of the opening game comeback or the great pace. No, indeed, every conversation was about how the Oilers would cope without Dwayne Roloson and whether it would be Ty Conklin or Jussi Markkanen who would start game two and, possibly, the rest of the series.

There were reasons to play or not play both. Since acquiring Roloson, coach Craig MacTavish played Roloson in every game but one, the final game of the regular season when Conklin started. This was only because the Oilers had clinched a playoff spot. While it might have been easy to criticize MacTavish for leaning so heavily on one man, the playoff race was so tight that he had no choice but to go with his best every night just to get into the post-season. Thus, both Conklin and Markkanen were decidedly rusty by the time the finals rolled around.

One could have argued to play Conklin, to allow the goalie to atone for the horrible mistake that ended game one. The flip side was just as convincing, though—to sit him because his confidence would be ruined by that mistake.

Markkanen was not so tainted by negative confidence, so he should start, the other argument suggested. But, he hadn't played a game since March 1. At least Conklin played that final regular season game and half a period two nights ago.

In the end, MacTavish elected to start Markkanen, and although the goalie was not the reason the Oilers lost 5–0, Markkanen also didn't steal a win for his team as it very much needed by this time. However, the real reason the Oilers lost game two was because of the goalie at the other end, Cam Ward. Despite the psychological difficulty of playing without Roloson—the main reason the Oilers were playing in the finals at all—they were the better team, created more great scoring chances, and had the majority of play. They simply couldn't beat Ward.

The Oilers had by far the better of play in the first, yet they got stung on a two-on-one and wound up trailing 1–0 after 20 minutes. Andrew Ladd and Eric Staal headed down the ice on an odd-man rush, and Ladd decided to shoot when defenceman Marc-Andre Bergeron slid back to block the passing lane. Unluckily, Ladd's shot hit Bergeron in the skate and flew past Markkanen in a direction the goalie couldn't anticipate.

Carolina went up 2–0 in the second period on a power play. No sooner had the Oilers finished killing off a 5-on-3 than Raffi Torres took a third straight Edmonton penalty, and on the ensuing 5-on-4, Frantisek Kaberle beat Markkanen with a shot from the point that the goalie should have had.

The turning point came late in the period, though, when the Oilers played a sloppy final shift of the second period in their own end.

Andrew Ladd's shot bounces of the skate of Marc-Andre Bergeron (out of frame) and past Jussi Markkanen for the first goal of the game.

Amidst a pile of players in front of him, Carolina goalie Cam Ward makes a spectacular save off a Shawn Horcoff shot.

Not fighting with the necessary urgency, they allowed Cory Stillman to stand alone in the slot in front of Markkanen. When he got the puck, he made no mistake on the backhand with less than three seconds on the clock. That was, as they say, the straw that broke the camel's back.

The third period was simply a more charged and pumped Carolina team taking advantage of a down-and-out Oilers squad. Edmonton took four minor penalties and a five-minute major to Georges Laraque, playing some eight minutes short-handed in total in the third period alone. Carolina struck twice more with the extra man, one goal by Doug Weight and another by Mark Recchi, and the Hurricanes waltzed away with a 5–0 whitewash in a game that was much closer than the score indicated.

Nonetheless, Carolina was leading 2–0 in a best-of-seven series heading back to Edmonton. Only one team in the history of this format (the 1942 Leafs) had ever rallied from 3–0 down, so if the Oilers had any hope of winning the Cup, they knew they had better win that pivotal third game at Rexall Place.

Doug Weight's goal early in the third added insult to injury for the Oilers.

Game Three
June 10, 2006
Carolina 1 at Edmonton 2

It wasn't pretty, but it was effective, and in the Edmonton dressing room after the game that's all that mattered. Ryan Smyth scored the game-winning goal when he went to the net and had the puck hit the shaft of his stick as he tried to avoid colliding with goalie Cam Ward. The puck bobbled toward the goal line, and by the time it crossed the red line Ward was down and Smyth was holding the crossbar to maintain balance. Video review confirmed the goal at 17:45 of the third period, and the Oilers won a critical game to fight their way back into the series.

In some respects, it was a deserved win; in others, a bit lucky. Yes, Edmonton was the better team,

Shawn Horcoff's deflection eludes goalie Cam Ward for the game's first goal early in the first period.

Ryan Smyth deflects the puck past Ward as he goes to the net, the game winner coming late in the third period.

but it went 0–7 on the power play again, including a 5-on-3 in the first for a minute and a half, and sooner or later the ineffective power play was bound to take its toll. By the same token, Carolina went 0–5 with the extra man and one goal either way would have made a world of difference in the game.

The home crowd gave the Oilers a tremendous ovation when they came onto the ice to start the game, and the players gave them something to cheer about less than three minutes in. A Jaroslav Spacek point shot was deftly deflected in front by Shawn Horcoff and the puck slid between Ward's pads for the all-important first goal of the game just 2:31 in.

The fans turned on the Oilers quickly, though, when they failed to produce any decent scoring chances—let alone goals—on the extended 5-on-3, and most of the rest of the game was tense, back-and-forth hockey. A key moment came soon after Horcoff's goal as a bad line change allowed Justin Williams to walk in alone on Jussi Markkanen. Williams tried to be too perfect, though, and drilled a shot over the net. At times, it looked like the Oilers were trying to sit on the lead, and when that happened the Hurricanes became dangerous. At other times, the Oilers attacked in earnest to score the second goal, only to be foiled time and again by Ward.

The best news for Edmonton fans, though, was that their own goalie, Markkanen, performed as well as Ward and made several fine saves to keep the game 1–0. Most important, he showed poise and handled the pressure-filled game with a maturity that clearly re-assured the players in front of him. Of course, the fact that Chris Pronger played nearly 29 minutes only helped the goalie, for Pronger was dominant, with the puck and without, inside his own blueline.

As the first period played out, and then second, and third, it looked

as though the Oilers would, in fact, win the game 1–0, but midway through the third Carolina captain Rod Brind'Amour silenced the crowd with a goal on an odd play. He took a quick snap shot in the slot, but the puck was blocked awkwardly by captain Jason Smith who was hit high in the chest but below the throat. As Smith turned in pain, the puck came directly back to Brind'Amour and he unleashed a second shot that beat Markkanen to the blocker side.

It took the Oilers a couple of minutes to compose themselves, but then they started to press for a second goal. Smyth came in over

the Carolina blueline on the right wing, dropped the puck back to Ales Hemsky and headed for the net. Hemsky passed to Smyth who was looking toward Ward and didn't see the puck, but it bounced up, hit his stick, and trickled in with just 2:15 left in the game. The Oilers won to live another day, and they could take a number of positives into game four. They managed to negate the Carolina offence for the most part. They negated the Hurricanes' potent power play. And, they played well with the lead. The question now was, could they do it again and tie the series two nights later.

Goalie Jussi Markkanen leaves the ice after a stellar performance under pressure to get the Oilers back into the series.

Game Four

June 12, 2006

Carolina 2 at Edmonton 1

Eric Staal, the leading point getter in the playoffs, had been unusually quiet in the finals until this night when he chose an opportune time to make a great play. Late in the second period of a 1–1 game, he knocked a puck out of mid air in the Edmonton end, made a great pass to teammate Mark Recchi, and watched as Recchi outwaited goalie Jussi Markkanen before scoring the game-winning goal. The win put Carolina within a game of the Stanley Cup as the teams headed back to Raleigh for game five.

It was a game in which Edmonton showed the effects of playing against a Canes team that blocked shots and received star goaltending. Time and again the Oilers refused to take the simple shot, instead choosing to try to make a perfect pass or circling along the boards instead of going to the net. The tentative Oilers were outdone again by a power play that looked to operate without a shred of confidence, again failing on a lengthy 5-on-3 in the first period when they could have taken charge of the game. In all, they were 0–5 with the extra man and were now 0–18 in the previous three games.

The Oilers got on the board first on a great play, albeit one that spoke to their lack of confidence in shooting. Sergei Samsonov carried the puck in over the Carolina line on a 3-on-2 rush and with a great chance to shoot he twirled and made an elaborate back pass to left winger Radek Dvorak. Samsonov broke free from his check and went to the net, and Dvorak made a beautiful pass that Samsonov merely redirected past goalie Cam Ward. It was to be the only time this combination passing worked all night.

The lead was short-lived. On the ensuing faceoff after the goal, Raffi Torres tripped his man at centre ice and was sent to the penalty

Sergei Samsonov's tip of the puck gets by Carolina goalie Cam Ward for the game's first goal.

box. Exactly 12 seconds later, the Hurricanes tied the score, doing on the power play what the Oilers time and again failed to do. Frantisek Kaberle's cross-ice pass to Cory Stillman was one-timed to perfection, beating Markkanen who was a bit slow to get from post to post.

The turning point in the game came a few minutes later when the Oilers had a long 5-on-3 with Ray Whitney and Aaron Ward in the penalty box. Chris Pronger was slow or inaccurate with his point shots, and the forwards failed to make quick, crisp passes to spring a man open for a clear shot. The period ended 1–1, but clearly by weathering the storm the Hurricanes were in a better position.

Jussi Markkanen makes one of several fine saves during a busy second period.

The second period started poorly for the Oilers as Carolina had several good scoring chances. Markkanen played his best at this stage, keeping the score tied and getting a bit lucky when Rod Brind'Amour hit the crossbar after deking the goalie out of position. Then Staal made his amazing pass to Recchi, and with the lead the Hurricanes sat back and battened the proverbial hatches.

Try as they might, the Oilers had trouble getting good shots on Ward in the final twenty minutes when they were desperate for a goal. They were able to control the puck, even bring it in to the Carolina end, but they had countless shots blocked or passes tipped, and Ward had very few saves to make.

The win gave the 'Canes a chance to win the Cup on home ice, while the Oilers had their toughest game yet ahead of them, having to break the stifling defence of their opponents to break through for some goals. They had scored just three times in as many games after beating Ward four times in the first game, but Carolina was playing in a way that suggested championship more than choke.

Mark Recchi scores the go-ahead goal late in the second period after a great pass from Eric Staal.

Game Five
June 14, 2006
Edmonton 4 at Carolina 3 (OT)

The Stanley Cup was in the building and the Carolina Hurricanes had all the momentum needed to claim it. The Edmonton Oilers, however, forced a game six when Fernando Pisani scored a short-handed goal at 3:31 of overtime to cancel the celebrations in Raleigh. Until that goal, it had been another dismal night for the Oilers' special teams. All of Carolina's goals were scored with the extra man, and Edmonton scored just once on seven chances.

The Oilers stunned the Carolina crowd with a goal on the first shift, just 16 seconds from the faceoff. They took the puck deep, and after a scrum in front the puck came back to Chris Pronger at the point. He wired a shot through a maze of players, beating Cam Ward who didn't see the puck.

That start only seemed to awaken the Hurricanes, though. The Oilers took three successive minor penalties, and Carolina capitalized on two of that number, both with Matt Greene in the box. On the first, Eric Staal had three shots, goalie Jussi Markkanen stopping the first two but not the third, a rebound while the goalie was belly on the ice.

Less than five minutes later, Ray Whitney clicked with Greene in the box when he wired a shot past a screened Markkanen, but after this the Oilers rallied instead of crumbled. They finally got their first power-play chance at 11:40, and Ales Hemsky converted. He took a Dick Tarnstrom pass from the point off to Ward's

Chris Pronger's shot beats goalie Cam Ward just 16 seconds into the game to stake Edmonton to an early 1-0 lead.

right and drilled a one-timer high to the short side to tie the game, 2-2. It was a huge morale booster for the team, as it was the first power-play goal in the last 19 chances.

The Oilers went to the dressing room with a 3-2 lead thanks to Michael Peca in the final minute. He circled Ward's net with the puck and was checked in front. Ales Hemsky got a shot away, though. Ward made the save, but Peca was right there to flip home the rebound to give the team confidence for the first time since game one.

That confidence took a big hit midway through the second period as a result of another power-play goal from Carolina. Ray Whitney's point shot bounced off the end boards and under Markkanen, who went down on the shot, and he appeared to have smothered the puck. The referees felt differently, however, and Eric Staal jammed at the goalie's pads until the puck wiggled free and into the net to tie the game, 3-3. The rest of the period was end-to-end, but there was a nervous sense of anticipation that the next goal would be the game winner.

That sense intensified in the third period. The Oilers had the better of play overall, but more important they had two early power-play chances. They weren't dangerous on either, however, but they continued to play with confidence. In the end, neither team could score the decisive goal, and for the first time in this finals, the teams headed to overtime.

The Oilers had all the chances in the short OT, but their fortunes went from horrible to amazing in half a minute. The horrible happened when Steve Staios was given a marginal tripping penalty at 3:03, and the amazing occurred half a minute later. Coming out of his own end on the power play, Carolina's Cory Stillman made a weak pass through the centre of the ice to Eric Staal. It never got there. Fernando Pisani

Eric Staal jams the puck out from under Jussi Markkanen and into the net to tie the score, 3-3.

Fernando Pisani rips a shot over the glove of Cam Ward to score a short-handed goal in overtime to force game six.

poked the puck free at the 'Canes blueline, controlled it, and went in alone on Ward. He buried a beautiful snap shot over the goalie's glove to empty the Oilers' bench and send the Carolina fans home disappointed.

And the Stanley Cup? Well, it wasn't going anywhere just yet.

Game Six
June 17, 2006
Carolina 0 at Edmonton 4

The Stanley Cup was in the building again, but the only team that played like a champion was the team that wasn't in a position to win. Jussi Markkanen stopped 16 mostly harmless Carolina shots, and the Oilers scored three times on the power play to force this once lop-sided series to a seventh game, winner take all.

For the first time, there were significant lineup changes for this game. Carolina had to scratch Doug Weight, whose shoulder injury suffered the previous game was not sufficiently healed, and in his place was Erik Cole, a stunning starter. Cole injured his neck three months ago and was cleared by doctors to play only the previous day. Coach Peter Laviolette hoped the insertion of Cole would add more offence, but, more importantly, inspire the rest of the team. It didn't, on both counts.

The game started polar opposite to gave five, neither team able to score in the opening 20 minutes and scoring chances few and far between. The Oilers, however, had the decided edge in play and were the vastly more physical of the teams. Raffi Torres threw his body every which way, and Michael Peca, Fernando Pisani, and the rest of the team followed suit.

The Oilers took the first penalty and then had two of their own power plays, but nothing amounted at either end. Perhaps the finest chance of the period came midway through when Edmonton goalie Jussi Markkanen came well out of his net to poke a puck out of harm's way. He succeeded, but Carolina picked up the loose puck at the blueline with Markkanen on his belly. Two great defensive plays kept the game scoreless.

The first 15 minutes of the second period were controlled by the Oilers. They helped their own cause by converting on an early power play

Crash, boom, bang! Edmonton's Ethan Moreau welcomes Carolina's Erik Cole back to action after three months off with a thundering check early in the first period to set the tone.

when Fernando Pisani took a pass in the slot from Ales Hemsky at the point on his backhand and let go a quick shot. Carolina defenceman Glen Wesley accidentally deflected the puck over the glove of his goalie Cam Ward, and the Oilers had the first goal of the game at 1:45. It was a slim, but well deserved, lead.

The Oilers kept coming, wave after wave on the forecheck, hitting the Carolina defencemen every shift, every touch of the puck. In its own end, Edmonton was tenacious on the puck carrier and moved the puck up ice smoothly. The team got its second goal thanks to a great rush and great tenacity by Peca. He carried the puck down the left wing and was checked off the puck behind the Hurricanes net. He stripped the defenceman of the puck, however, and it came back to the point where Steve Staios took a quick shot. This time it was Raffi Torres in front who deflected the puck beautifully between Ward's pads, and the Oilers had their first two-goal lead since game one.

With about five minutes to go, the Hurricanes were being outshot 21–3, including 11–0 in the second. Laviolette called a timeout, and his team responded, getting the better of the play the last five minutes and causing two Edmonton penalties. The Oilers withstood the attack, though, and headed to the dressing room up 2–0.

In the final period, they pulled away in dominating fashion, but not without a moment of discomfort. Edmonton had a 3-on-1, and the final pass to Radek Dvorak saw the shooter have an empty net. Dvorak made the shot and raised his arms to celebrate his goal only to see Ward make the save of the year, reaching back with the glove to keep the game 2–0. The save actually deflated the Oilers for a few minutes, but they got a power play soon after and converted on it. Ryan Smyth took a Michael Peca pass at the Carolina blueline and

Radek Dvorak is stopped cold by Cam Ward, the most amazing save of the entire playoffs to keep the score 2-0 early in the third period.

Carolina goalie Cam Ward recomposes himself after the Oilers scored in the third period to make it 4-0.

skated down the left side, cut into the middle on his backhand and beat Ward to the near side to make it 3–0. Dvorak finished the scoring on another power-play rush, making a great pass to Shawn Horcoff who was driving to the net. Horcoff drilled a quick shot past Ward, and the crowd went crazy realizing a game seven was now inevitable.

By the end of the game, Carolina had been badly outhit, outscored, and outplayed, and although the Hurricanes were going home for the final game it was the Oilers that had the decided advantage now.

Game Seven
June 19, 2006
Edmonton at Carolina

The Carolina Hurricanes blew two chances to win the Cup, but they didn't blow a third chance, beating Edmonton 3–1 to claim their first championship in franchise history.

For the Oilers, it was a heart-breaking effort, as close as you can come to winning without actually doing so.

The Hurricanes came out and played an Edmonton-style first period, crashing and banging into everything in an opposing sweater, going to the net, and moving the puck crisply out of their own end. They were rewarded early on after what seemed like a harmless turnover by Steve Staios at centre ice. The Hurricanes took the puck deep into the Oilers' end and goalie Jussi Markkanen made a great save off Matt Cullen, but as the puck came around the boards defenceman Aaron Ward took a quick shot from the point that

Chris Pronger nails Mark Recchi along the boards in the Edmonton end.

Frantisek Kaberle's point shot on the power play deflects off defenceman Jason Smith and past goalie Jussi Markkanen.

Carolina captain Rod Brind'Amour lifts the Stanley Cup for the first time in his long and distinguished career.

went through sticks and skates and, finally, through Markkanen's pads for a 1–0 lead just 1:26 into the game.

The Oilers woke up with that early score and went on the attack, having better puck possession the rest of the period but not getting many close-in chances on Cam Ward in the Carolina net.

The period ended on a strange play. Ethan Moreau took a penalty deep in the Carolina end, but the Hurricanes, in control, brought the puck up ice. They got a shot on goal that bounced in the air behind Markkanen and came close to the line, but Staios fell on the puck in the crease. Referee Brad Watson signaled penalty shot, but the second referee, Bill McCreary, corrected the call by pointing out that as soon as Staios touched the puck, the delayed penalty was over and play dead. This all with just five seconds left in the first period.

Still, that meant the Oilers started the second a man down. It may have been the turning point in the game, even though they killed that penalty off in spades. The two best scoring chances were both by the Oilers. Fernando Pisani had a partial breakaway, but he whistled a shot way over the net. Moments later, Rem Murray had a chance right in front only to be stoned by Ward. A goal by either player would have tied the game, 1–1. Instead, it was Carolina that composed itself and scored the next goal.

Jaroslav Spacek took a penalty at 4:10, and just eight seconds later Frantisek Kaberle's point shot bounced off a sliding Jason Smith, changed directions, and beat Markkanen. The rest of the period was controlled by the Hurricanes, and the Oilers couldn't muster any shots, even on a 5-on-3 late in the period.

The Oilers came streaking out to start the third period and made it a one-goal game at 1:03 thanks to Pisani. Raffi Torres skated down the left wing and took a simple shot at Ward. He steered the puck away, and Murray got one crack at it before Pisani knocked the loose puck over the fallen Ward. The chase for the Cup was on in earnest now.

The period was up-and-down, back-and-forth with an intensity unseen before in the series. First, Carolina came close to going up by two again, then the Oilers had the better of play. They also got a late power play when Bret Hedican took a roughing penalty at 12:38, but they couldn't beat Ward. Justin Williams closed out the scoring with an empty-net goal at 18:59, and the celebrations in Raleigh began. The Carolina Hurricanes had won the Stanley Cup, but the Edmonton Oilers had won the hearts of Canada with their amazing season.

All-Time Playoff Record

YEAR	GP	W-L	GF	GA
1979–80	3	0–3	6	12
1980–81	9	5–4	35	35
1981–82	5	2–3	23	27
1982–83	16	11–5	80	50
1983–84	19	15–4	94	56
1984–85	18	15–3	98	57
1985–86	10	6–4	41	30
1986–87	21	16–5	87	57
1987–88	18	16–2	84	53
1988–89	7	3–4	20	25
1989–90	22	16–6	93	60
1990–91	18	9–9	57	60
1991–92	16	8–8	49	54
1992–93		DNQ		
1993–94		DNQ		
1994–95		DNQ		
1995–96		DNQ		
1996–97	12	5–7	32	37
1997–98	12	5–7	24	25
1998–99	4	0–4	7	11
1999–2000	5	1–4	11	14
2000–01	6	2–4	13	16
2001–02		DNQ		
2002–03	6	2–4	11	20
2003–04		DNQ		
2004–05		NO SEASON		
2005–06	24	15–9	69	60
TOTALS	251	152–99	934	759

Perhaps Mark Messier's crowning glory in Edmonton came in the spring of 1990 when he led the Oilers to a surprise fifth Cup.

Stanley Cup Finals Appearances

1983

May 10	NY Islanders 2 at Edmonton 0
May 12	NY Islanders 6 at Edmonton 3
May 14	Edmonton 1 at NY Islanders 5
May 17	Edmonton 2 at NY Islanders 4

NY Islanders win Stanley Cup 4–0

1984

May 10	Edmonton 1 at NY Islanders 0
May 12	Edmonton 1 at NY Islanders 6
May 15	NY Islanders 2 at Edmonton 7
May 17	NY Islanders 2 at Edmonton 7
May 19	NY Islanders 2 at Edmonton 5

Edmonton wins Stanley Cup 4–1

1985

May 21	Edmonton 1 at Philadelphia 4
May 23	Edmonton 3 at Philadelphia 1
May 25	Philadelphia 3 at Edmonton 4
May 28	Philadelphia 3 at Edmonton 5
May 30	Philadelphia 3 at Edmonton 8

Edmonton wins Stanley Cup 4–1

1987

May 17	Philadelphia 2 at Edmonton 4
May 20	Philadelphia 2 at Edmonton 3 (Kurri 6:50 OT)
May 22	Edmonton 3 at Philadelphia 5
May 24	Edmonton 4 at Philadelphia 1
May 26	Philadelphia 4 at Edmonton 3
May 28	Edmonton 2 at Philadelphia 3
May 31	Philadelphia 1 at Edmonton 3

Edmonton wins Stanley Cup 4–3

1988

May 18	Boston 1 at Edmonton 2
May 20	Boston 2 at Edmonton 4
May 22	Edmonton 6 at Boston 3
May 24	Edmonton 3 at Boston 3 (suspended due to power failure)
May 26	Boston 3 at Edmonton 6

Edmonton wins Stanley Cup 4–0

1990

May 15	Edmonton 3 at Boston 2 (Klima 55:13 OT)
May 18	Edmonton 7 at Boston 2
May 20	Boston 2 at Edmonton 1
May 22	Boston 1 at Edmonton 5
May 24	Edmonton 4 at Boston 1

Edmonton wins Stanley Cup 4–1

Jari Kurri makes the back door pass to Wayne Gretzky as goalie Ron Hextall tries to react to the play.

Recalling the 1989–90 Edmonton Oilers

By the time the 1989–90 season got under way, the pendulum had swung far away from the Oilers of the mid-1980s that had won four Stanley Cups in five years.

For starters, owner Peter Pocklington had traded the great Wayne Gretzky to Los Angeles in the summer of 1988. Second, during the playoffs at the end of that inaugural, Gretzky-less season (1988–89), Gretzky and his new team, the Kings, had eliminated the Oilers in seven games, giving greater sense that it was Gretzky more than his teammates who had been the most important ingredient to those four Cups with the Oilers.

But captain Mark Messier, who had inherited the "C" after 99's departure, instilled in his team a greater sense of belief as the '89–'90 season began, in part through his words, in part

through his deeds. By the time the second regular season of the post-Gretzky era had ended, Messier placed second in scoring with 129 points, second only to Gretzky's 142 with the Kings. But Edmonton's record of 38–28–14 was notably superior to Los Angeles which finished five games under .500 at 34–39–7.

In the 1990 playoffs, both the Kings and Oilers dispatched their first-round opponents, setting up a rematch of the previous year—Gretzky's new and current team versus his great alma mater. Messier made sure there would be no defeat. He led the Oilers to a 7–0 hammering in the first game, and the Kings never recovered, losing in four straight.

Edmonton went on to beat Chicago in six games to set up a Cup finals with Boston, hardly a matchup many would

have predicted at the start of the season. Again, it was the first game that set the tone. Edmonton led after two periods by 2–0, but the Bruins tied the game late in the third to send it into overtime. Petr Klima scored later in the third extra period, a win that elevated the spirits of the Oilers and deflated those of the Bruins who had fought so hard to tie the game.

Game two started out the same way. The Oilers led 2–0; the Bruins tied the game, this time early in the second period. Edmonton woke up, however, and scored four times before 40 minutes had been played, and the team coasted to a 7–2 victory. Although the Bruins won game three by a close 2–1 score, the Oilers blew the series open with a 5–1 win two nights later and captured their fifth Cup with another dominating win in Boston, 4–1, on May 24, 1990. Bill Ranford was brilliant in goal for Edmonton, and the attack was led by Craig Simpson and Jari Kurri, both of whom had eight points in the five-game finals. It was a surprise win, to be sure, but a win that authenticated the importance of team play over individual stardom. For all his greatness and records, Gretzky never won a Cup after 1988 when he left Edmonton. Messier won in 1990 and again four years later with the New York Rangers on a team with several Oilers from this special class of 1990.

The Oilers last won the Cup in 1990, which also represents the last time a Canadian team won Lord Stanley's trophy.

The Gretzky File

Although Wayne Gretzky played just 696 regular season games with Edmonton, the records he set have yet to be touched by any NHL player. Here is a small sampling of his greatest accomplishments while with the Oil.

In those 696 games, he had 472 multiple-point games. He recorded eight points twice, seven points six times, and five points a whopping 57 times.

The fewest points he recorded in a year was 137 in 1979–80. The most was 215 in 1985–86. Four times he scored more than 200 points in a year, the only player ever to do it even once.

He leads the all-time Oilers list in goals (583), assists (1,086), points (1,669), hat tricks (43), and short-handed goals (55). Four times he scored five goals in a game.

By the time he retired, Gretzky held more than 50 NHL records, many of which he established while with the Oilers. He scored 92 goals in the 1981–82 season and had 163 assists in '85–'86. Twice he had an incredible ten hat tricks in a year (1981–82 and 1983–84). In 1984–85, he had 255 points, regular season and playoffs. At the 1983 All-Star Game he scored four goals in the third period, another record.

Gretzky's playoff record is also second to none. He leads the all-time list in goals (122), assists (260), and points (382), as well as most career hat tricks (ten), and most points in one playoff year (47, in 1984–85).

Wayne Gretzky is mobbed by teammates after scoring his 77th goal of the season on February 24, 1982, to set a new NHL record for goals in a season.

Edmonton Oilers' Honour Roll

Hall of Famers
Glen Sather (1997)
Wayne Gretzky (1999)
Jari Kurri (2001)
Grant Fuhr (2003)
Paul Coffey (2004)

Trophy Winners
Conn Smythe Trophy
Mark Messier (1983–84)
Wayne Gretzky (1984–85, 1987–88)
Bill Ranford (1989–90)

Art Ross Trophy
Wayne Gretzky (1980–81, 1981–82,
   1982–83, 1983–84, 1984–85,
   1985–86, 1986–87)

Hart Trophy
Wayne Gretzky (1979–80, 1980–81,
   1981–82, 1982–83, 1983–84,
   1984–85, 1985–86, 1986–87)
Mark Messier (1989–90)

Lester B. Pearson Award
Wayne Gretzky (1981–82, 1982–83,
   1983–84, 1984–85, 1986–87)
Mark Messier (1989–90)

Norris Trophy
Paul Coffey (1984–85, 1985–86)

Vezina Trophy
Grant Fuhr (1987–88)

Lady Byng Trophy
Wayne Gretzky (1979–80)
Jari Kurri (1984–85)

King Clancy Trophy
Kevin Lowe (1989–90)

Jack Adams Award
Glen Sather (1985–86)

Retired Numbers
99—Wayne Gretzky
31—Grant Fuhr
17—Jari Kurri
7—Paul Coffey
3—Al Hamilton

Captains
Ron Chipperfield (1979–80)
Blair MacDonald/Lee Fogolin
   (1980–81)
Lee Fogolin (1981–83)
Wayne Gretzky (1983–88)
Mark Messier (1988–91)
Kevin Lowe (1991–92)
Craig MacTavish (1992–94)
Shayne Corson (1994–95)
Kelly Buchberger (1995–99)
Doug Weight (1999–2001)
Jason Smith (2001–06)

Coaches
Glen Sather (1979–80)
Bryan Watson/Glen Sather
   (1980–81)
Glen Sather (1981–89)
John Muckler (1989–91)
Ted Green (1991–93)
Ted Green/Glen Sather (1993–94)
George Burnett/Ron Low (1994–95)
Ron Low (1995–99)
Kevin Lowe (1999–2000)
Craig MacTavish (2000–2006)

All-Star Team Selections
1979–80
Wayne Gretzky, centre (2nd team)

1980–81
Wayne Gretzky, centre (1st team)

1981–82
Wayne Gretzky, centre (1st team)
Mark Messier, left wing (1st team)
Grant Fuhr, goal (2nd team)
Paul Coffey, defence (2nd team)

1982–83
Wayne Gretzky, centre (1st team)
Mark Messier, left wing (1st team)
Paul Coffey, defence (2nd team)

1983–84
Wayne Gretzky, centre (1st team)
Mark Messier, left wing (2nd team)
Paul Coffey, defence (2nd team)
Jari Kurri, right wing (2nd team)

1984–85
Wayne Gretzky, centre (1st team)
Paul Coffey, defence (1st team)
Jari Kurri, right wing (1st team)

1985–86
Wayne Gretzky, centre (1st team)
Paul Coffey, defence (1st team)
Jari Kurri, right wing (2nd team)

1986–87
Wayne Gretzky, centre (1st team)
Jari Kurri, right wing (1st team)

1987–88
Grant Fuhr, goal (1st team)
Wayne Gretzky, centre (2nd team)

1988–89
Jari Kurri, right wing (2nd team)

1989–90
Mark Messier, centre (1st team)

1990–2006